Recognition for

The Perpetual Retirement Income Machine

Income is the number one issue for almost everyone planning or already in retirement. The PRIM solution is well thought out, data driven, and can make a huge positive difference in the success of any retirement plan.

Skip Kelley, *Financial Advisor,*
Safe Money Retirement Specialists, Manchester NH

This book is very well written, explaining complex issues in an understandable way. Using wrap-ups at the end of each chapter is effective! This is a very valuable educational tool.

Robert D. O'Reilly, *Retired Senior VP,*
BBVA Compass Bank

There was a time when companies that employed us took care of creating safe retirements for us. Those times are gone. In our journey to a secure retirement, we are increasingly on our own. And maintaining the "gold" in our golden years is a tough job requiring a keen intellect, nerves of steel and persistent follow-up. But what if we could build a machine that leaves the driving to it? Welcome to the realm of the PRIM!

Jim Swift, *retired KXAN broadcast journalist*

Using a classic and time-tested investment methodology with updated knowledge, Scott Campbell and Steve Lewit have published a must-read for anyone that wishes to understand how to build a retirement plan without worry. A great commonsense approach to retirement planning!

Uriah Zane Hunt, *Co-Founder/Owner Via 313*

An interesting guide that describes various ways of allocating investments using the PRIM approach. The PRIM approach can help any retiree build a plan that preserves assets and reduces risk, leading to a less stressful retirement experience.

Jerome Kruemcke, *Certified Public Accountant*

The concepts and strategies of the PRIM approach are invaluable tools upon which to build a sound retirement income plan. They have proven, over the years, to be indispensable allies for me in helping my clients achieve confidence and peace of mind for their retirement years.

Tami Simpson, *CFP®,*
Wealth Financial Group West, Costa Mesa CA

The Perpetual Retirement Income Machine is essential reading for anyone thinking about or planning their retirement. Far and away the most complete and easy to understand income strategies for people with virtually all levels of assets and income needs. This is not a pie-in-the-sky approach with fictional promises that never come true. This is a down-to-earth approach that works. What more could anyone ask for?

Dauphinais Poe, *Founder, CEO,*
DFW Retirement Planners, Fort Worth TX

The Perpetual Retirement Income Machine offers proven strategies which will give you peace of mind and confidence about your retirement income. It is a must read for anyone who wants to be sure that they will never outlive their income and assets, and at the same time, assure that they maintain their lifestyle throughout their retirement years.

Steve Casto, *Financial Advisor,*
Retirement Matters, Omaha NE

This book can show almost anyone how to create a retirement income plan that successfully manages all the key retirement income risks and dangers. Because it is so comprehensive and effective, it builds confidence that your income and quality of life will be sustained throughout your retirement years. A great book to read.

Bryan Lunt, *Partner,*
Hamilton Partners, Itasca IL

Steve and Scott have done a terrific job in writing the PRIM book. Their idea of building an income machine that creates retirement income day after day and year after year is nothing short of visionary. I've seen how good income planning is life changing. The PRIM approach is better than good income planning, it is terrific income planning.

Len Hayduchok, *President, Financial Advisor,*
Dedicated Senior Advisors, Hamilton NJ

With all the market and economic uncertainty surrounding us today, this book presents a sound and proven income approach for retirement. I have seen how these strategies have changed the lives of my clients. I suggest all consider using them.

Roger Cowen, *CEO, Financial Advisor,*
Cowen Tax and Advisory Services, W. Hartford CT

The answer to the problem of having sufficient and enduring retirement income is solved in *The Perpetual Retirement Income Machine*. It makes a complex subject easy to understand and provides a foundation for planning which virtually everyone should consider using.

Nick Sloane, *Financial Advisor,*
Sloane Wealth Management, Warrenville IL

Everyone should read *The Perpetual Retirement Income Machine* and learn how to build their personal PRIM. It will allow you to take charge of your finances and build a retirement income cash flow upon which you can absolutely count on.

Thomas Chrobak, *Financial Advisor, College Planner,*
Chrobak Advisory, Chicago IL

While nothing is perfect, the PRIM approach comes pretty close. This is a no-nonsense, down to earth, step-by-step planning strategy that is sure to deliver excellent results. Everyone should read this book.

Dan Cuprill, *Advisor Architect Creator*
Matson Caprill Financial Consultants, Cincinnati OH

If you're interested in creating retirement income that will last—*READ THIS BOOK NOW!* Simply the best book on the subject that I've read in years.

Barbara Traylor Smith, *CEO,*
Retirement Outfitters, Grand Junction CO

The PRIM approach is light years ahead of how most financial planners plan income for their retirement clients. Anyone considering their retirement should read this book and build their own PRIM.

Jack Hradesky, *President,*
Tax-Free Retirement Specialist, Marina Del Rey CA

Anyone who understands just how difficult it is to plan retirement income will appreciate the wisdom of the PRIM approach. Lewit and Campbell have taken a complex, challenging subject and created a strategy that is simple to understand and effective in its delivery. My clients sleep well at night, knowing that their PRIM will produce income they can count on for the rest of their lives.

Ross Brown, *Financial Advisor*
Iron Gate Advisory, St. Charles IL

The Perpetual Retirement Income Machine

Never worry about your income again

Steve Lewit and Scott Campbell

The Perpetual Retirement Income Machine:
Never Worry About Your Income Again

This publication is designed to provide accurate and authoritative information with regard to the subject matter covered. It is sold with the understanding that the publisher is not engaged in rendering legal, accounting, or other professional advice. If legal advice or other expert assistance is required it, the services of a competent professional should be sought.

The information in this book is for general use and, while we believe the information is reliable and accurate, it is important to remember individual situations may be entirely different. Therefore, information should be relied upon only when coordinated with individual professional tax and/or financial advice. You need to consider your specific situation including your health and legacy goals before acting on any information present-ed in this book. Please note that neither the information presented nor any opinion expressed is to be considered as an offer to buy or purchase any insurance or securities products and services referenced in this book.

All figures and examples in this book are based on rates and assumptions no later in time than April 2017. Rates and assumptions are not guaranteed and may be subject to change. As in all assumptions and examples, individual results may vary based on a wide range of factors unique to each person's situation. All data provided in this book are to be used for informational purposes only. Any slights against individuals, companies, or organizations are unintentional.

The information provided is not intended as any investment or planning advice and is for educational purposes only. The idea of an income machine is for conceptual purposes only. While the production of income can have aspects which are mechanical in nature, there is no such thing a an income machine in real life. You assume full responsibility and risk of loss resulting from the use of this information. Steve Lewit and Scott Campbell will not be liable for any direct, special, indirect, incidental, consequential, or punitive damages or any other damages whatsoever, whether in an action based upon a statute, contract, tort, (including but not limited to negligence), or otherwise, relating to the use of this information. In no event will Steve Lewit or Scott Campbell, or their related partnerships or corporations, agents, or employees be liable to you or anyone else for any decision made or action taken in reliance on the information in this book or for any consequential, special, or similar damages, even if advised of the possibility of such damage.

Wishing You
the Richness of Life

Table of Contents

Introduction   1

Chapter 1 — Sleeping Well on Windy Nights   3

Chapter 2 — PRIM — A Different Way of Thinking   7

Chapter 3 — The Basic PRIM   15

Chapter 4 — PRIM Building and Your Personal Risk Style   23

Chapter 5 — The Key Retirement Income Risks   29
                   and Your Personal Risk Style

Chapter 6 — The Risk Taker's PRIM   45

Chapter 7 — Risk Avoiders PRIM   57

Chapter 8 — The Risk Manager's PRIM   71

Chapter 9 — Under The Hood of Your PRIM   89

Chapter 10 — A Few Final Words   99

Perpetual Retirement Income Machine (PRIM)
ESSENTIAL PARTS LIST

(1) 	Comes pre-fueled by Social Security. Some may want to further enchance this Driver's output.
(2) 	May be fueled at all production levels from Low to High Risk.
(3) 	Guarantees income you can't outlive.
(4) 	Preserves smooth running in all types of inclement conditions.
(5) 	Keeps income growing to offset increasing prices.
(6) 	Less taxes means more income.

PRIM parts are available in all sizes, each requiring a different type of fuel.

Parts may be configured to fit virtually any situation, making PRIM construction easily tailored to each individual's specific income requirements.

Note: All interest, growth, and inflation rates used throughout this book are for illustration purposes only and should not be construed as actual performance numbers.

INTRODUCTION

After a combined 43 years of working with retirees and those planning retirement, it is clear to us that creating sustainable income in retirement is the biggest challenge. The question we hear the most is, "Will I have enough?"

How that question is answered will either provide peace-of-mind about the future or foster uncertainty and fear. While everyone desires to be financially secure, we've found that most people have a deeper, more important desire: to put their head on their pillow at night and get a good night's sleep. They want peace of mind!

Is it possible to feel financially secure and have peace of mind in today's economic, political, and volatile market environment? Since we entered the business in the 1990s, we've seen huge obstacles that the average retiree has had to dodge. During that time, there have been political and economic turmoil, two significant market collapses—one in 2000 – 2001 and the other the financial meltdown of 2008—bank bailouts, quantitative easing, trade wars, world debt concerns, the collapse of oil and gas prices, skyrocketing health care expenses, and several wars.

Today, we have record stock market levels (at the time of writing the Dow was at 20,596 and the S&P at 2344, which many people feel are bubbles waiting to burst. Add to that the lowest interest rates in history, and the answer to the question of whether it's possible to feel financially secure and have peace of mind in today's world is, most often, a resounding ... NO!

When people retire from work, they don't retire with the need for a lump-sum of money. They retire with the need for sustainable income. Today, the creation of sustainable income is more challenging than ever. Those that fear the stock market are stuck with low performing interest rate products, or worse, they are sitting on the sidelines in cash. And for those who embrace the stock market to its fullest, they are forced to endure unavoidable volatility while withdrawing funds from their investments for needed income. These folks could put themselves on a high-risk collision course with income failure when the next big crash materializes.

Our passion, and the reason for writing this book, is to take the mystery and the myths of creating retirement income off the table. We want to show you how to build a system for income creation that is based on fact, rather than opinion, myths, or any other kind of fiction. When an income plan is built on substance, we know that your confidence will rise and your fear of the future will either be reduced or eliminated. The result is peace of mind—what all retirees desire and deserve.

We have assessed and used data and scientific evidence to build an income machine that can crank out spendable income for the rest of your life. We call this machine PRIM: Perpetual Retirement Income Machine. This book is about how you can build your own PRIM and give yourself the gift of a safe and secure retirement!

As you will see, because the PRIM approach to retirement planning is intellectually and scientifically sound, it creates emotional stability. Your PRIM will provide you with spendable income. More significantly, it will provide you with less stress, worry, concern, or fear of the unknown. At the end of the day, PRIM will allow you to sleep peacefully, knowing that your income can weather any storm.

We certainly hope you enjoy reading about the PRIM approach. More importantly, we hope that you build your own PRIM and that it helps make your retirement the success and joy it should be.

— Steve Lewit and Scott Campbell

CHAPTER 1

SLEEPING WELL ON WINDY NIGHTS

1

There once was a farmer out in the Midwest who needed a farmhand. He put an ad in the newspaper, and to his chagrin, he only got one response. However, having no other choice, he invited the young man in for an interview.

The young man looked nice enough, but when the farmer asked him if he had any farm work experience the boy only answered, "I sleep well on windy nights."

This puzzled the farmer so he asked him another question, "Do you know how to milk cows?"

The young man responded, "I sleep well on windy nights."

The farmer, having no one else to interview, asked him yet another question, "Have you had experience fixing tractors?"

Again, the young man responded, "I sleep well on windy nights."

And so it went, question after question answered exactly the same way.

Finally, the farmer, exasperated with the answers to his questions and frustrated that he had no other people to interview, hired the young man.

Things seemed to go well enough, that is, until one stormy night. While everyone slept, a high-wind storm swept across the farmland. The howling of the wind and banging of the shutters woke the farmer. Immediately he knew that the storm would soon be crashing down upon him and his farm.

The farmer rose to action, running down the hallway and banging on the young man's door yelling, "Wake up, wake up! A big storm is coming, and we need to make everything on the farm secure. Wake up! I'll meet you out by the barn."

And, indeed, the storm was now upon them. The farmer leaned into the wind as the rain poured down, and he raced into the barn. He needed to make sure things were in place and latched down. He looked around to see what needed to be done and noted that the windows were shuttered tight, all the tools were secure in their holders, there were no leaks in the roof and all was secure.

So, he left the barn and ran to the fields, angry that the young man had not risen to help him. When he reached the fields, he found all the hay baled and wired; all the fencing in place that secured his herd; and all the electrical wires tied safely in place.

Satisfied that his farm and livelihood were secure, the farmer went back to bed, still miffed at the young man for not rising to help during the storm.

The next morning the farmer was up having breakfast when the young man finally rose and joined him. The farmer greeted the young man curtly, "You know, we had a big storm last night. I banged on your door as we needed to check the barn, the fields, and the equipment to make sure all was secure, and you didn't show up. Why not?"

The young man looked at the farmer puzzled, "Do you remember what I told you when you hired me? I told you, I sleep well on windy nights ... and now you know why."

What is the moral of the story?

You are wise enough to know that there will be many windy nights throughout your retirement, especially when it comes to your income. The purpose of

Always remember—
It's not about the money,
it's about life!

this book is to make sure that you sleep as well as possible when those financial storms come your way, no matter their intensity.

At the end of the day, while money is important, life's not about money. Money, as you will soon see, is the fuel for your journey. It's the fuel that you will use in your retirement income machine to generate enough income for the rest of your life. To sleep well on windy nights, you must first purchase the correct parts to build your income machine, your PRIM.

The following chapters will show you exactly how to do just that.

CHAPTER 2

—PRIM—
A DIFFERENT WAY
OF THINKING

2

You are taught to save over your lifetime and build a retirement fund. Then you are taught to invest those funds to provide a suitable income stream that will last throughout your retirement years. Easier said than done, right? Especially now, when markets are considered overvalued, interest rates are rooted at historical lows, there is growing concern about world-wide political instability and an increasing threat of terrorism. As we write this book, China's economy continues to slow, the U.S. has elected a new president, the UK is trying to implement "Brexit," European debt crises endure, and new terrorist attacks have occurred in Istanbul, Baghdad, Quebec, Paris and Berlin.

> "Each day, 10,000 Baby Boomers retire and begin receiving Medicare and Social Security."
>
> Sen. Rob Portman, *The Wall Street Journal*

As financial advisors, we think about these problems all the time and how to navigate through them on behalf of our clients. With the arrival of the Baby Boomer generation into retirement age, there is a growing and substantial amount of research devoted to providing income solutions that will serve to navigate a potentially turbulent future. We now have many retirement income approaches from which to choose, and we've used most of them successfully with our clients.

But things have changed.

For example, until the early 2000's, preserving principal and living off interest rate products was a common retirement strategy. However, rates have dropped so low it has become almost impossible for the average retiree to generate enough income on interest alone. Today, with fixed rates ranging between 1% and 3%, you would need to be a millionaire just to generate $30,000 a year of spendable income. Given the current environment, living off interest alone is no longer a viable strategy.

Another strategy commonly employed was (and still is) creating income from dividends—why not invest in blue chip stocks and simply live off the dividend yield? This approach appeals to the individual who claims they don't necessarily care about the volatility of the underlying stock so long as the yield remains consistent. Unfortunately, over the years, we have found that because dividends are not guaranteed, they carry too much risk and uncertainty when it comes to producing reliable income. For example, consider the largest energy infrastructure company in North America, Kinder Morgan Inc. (KMI). On October 6, 2014, *The Motley Fool* (www.fool.com) posted an article titled "Is Kinder Morgan Inc. the Perfect Retirement Stock?" The article talked about how dividend growth stocks are, historically, the best performing class of investments and how this high-yielding energy company "might be able to help you fund your retirement in a comfortable, but sustainable manner."

The article went on to talk about how large, stable, and great Kinder Morgan was. They talked about how the dividend yield was "high, secure, and growing." The article's author (Adam Galas) even went so far to say that "Kinder Morgan has one of the best track records of meeting or beating dividend guidance of any stock I've ever seen!" Finally, to put a cherry on top of everything, he predicted that by 2020 the dividend yield would reach 8.3% based on the current price.

At the time the article was written, KMI was trading at $44.71 with a dividend of $1.92 per share, which is a yield of 4.2%. If at that time, you bought $100,000 worth of Kinder Morgan for your retirement income needs, expecting to receive $4,200 per year in spendable income, you would have been severely disappointed. By August 2016, the shares had fallen to $21.86 *and* the dividend was cut to $0.50 per share. Therefore, the value of your $100,000 would have fallen to $48,633 (-51%) and the dividend income would have fallen to $1,118 (-74%) annually.

Blue chip stocks like GE, Citibank, and Conagra Brands all have had dividend cuts and that's just the beginning of the list. Bottom line, because many dividend strategies come up short, they cannot be counted on to produce reliable retirement income.

What to do?

A short story.

We were giving a retirement income lecture to a small group of business executives from a local manufacturing company who were nearing retirement. The question on their minds was the same question most people asked, "How can I sustain my quality of life throughout retirement and not run out of money?"

We then began to explain different retirement income options; the pros and cons of each strategy and how our recommendations were backed by research and other evidence. After an hour or so of discussion, one of the executives stood up with a big smile and said, "Hold on guys. This is getting too complicated. Can't you just design a machine that cranks out income so that we can flip a switch and turn it on? You know, an income machine!"

While he was kidding (remember, he worked for a manufacturing company), we looked at each other and immediately knew what the other was thinking. Yes, we can build an income machine. So, that's what we did.

We named the machine: *PRIM—a Perpetual Retirement Income Machine.*

Since that time, we see ourselves as manufacturers as much as we see ourselves as financial advisors. When people ask us what we do, we answer that we are in manufacturing. When they ask what we manufacture, we answer, "Income machines."

Over the years, we've found that the concept of a *machine to pro-*

duce income has helped our clients see their retirement income challenges, and possible solutions, more clearly. When investments and financial strategies are thought of as machine parts, decisions about the types of products and strategies to use become more objective and much easier to make.

Most people we meet don't have any retirement plan at all. In fact, 77% of pre-retirees do not have a retirement income plan. And those that think they have a plan, often have nothing more than a hodgepodge of products and strategies designed by different advisors, from different perspectives, favoring different products. Do they work? Yes, to a degree. But do they work like a well-oiled machine? No!

Imagine for a moment you set out to build your own car. First you order tires from Cadillac, then a transmission from Honda, then a chassis from Ford, an engine from Volkswagen, a steering column from Chevy, and so on. Then you put these parts together to make your car. It may look something like this:

> **77% of pre-retirees do not have a retirement income plan.**
>
> Fundamentals of Retirement Planning
> Fidelity Investments 10.22.15

Chassis from Ford

Steering Column from Chevy

Tires from Cadillac

Engine from Volkswagon

Transmission from Honda

Will your car run? Yes, of course it will.

But, will it run at peak performance? No.

Will it cross the finish line in an endurance race?

Probably not, because it is a hodgepodge machine that was slapped together with disparate pieces, not a carefully assembled machine with parts that fit well, all meant to perform efficiently together at a high level.

When it comes to producing retirement income, most income plans are built much like this car: a piece from here, an idea from there, one person watching over your market money, another watching over your taxes, and yet another looking at your annuities or insurance. Unfortunately, when the going gets rough, these piecemeal solutions don't fare very well and may break down well before the end of the race.

Research shows that most people understand that their retirement plan is not built well. Only 39% of retirees felt "very confident" that they would have enough money to live comfortably throughout retirement. Unfortunately for the other 61%, sleeping on windy nights does not come easily.

When you follow our instructions and build your PRIM, you will be building a unified, well-planned, high-quality machine that creates retirement income year-after-year for the rest of your life. Your machine will get you through your personal retirement endurance race to the finish line with few worries, no matter how difficult the road becomes.

PRIMs are auto-piloted machines. Once set in motion, they need only minor adjustments as market, economic, and lifestyle needs change. Since PRIMs are machines, they are not emotionally affected like humans are in stressful situations (such as market downturns). They just do their job as planned: creating income that fits both your financial and emotional needs.

Let's begin your PRIM building journey.

Chapter 2 Wrap-Up

- [ ] **PRIM** — a *Perpetual Retirement Income Machine* that you can build to fit your personal income needs.

- [ ] Most people build their retirement income plan haphazardly (if they have a plan at all), which fosters anxiety and a lack of confidence about their future.

- [ ] Only 39% of retirees feel "very confident" that they will have enough money to live comfortably throughout retirement.

- [ ] The PRIM is an efficient income machine that can be set on auto-pilot

CHAPTER 3

THE BASIC PRIM

3

Your PRIM is a machine; it needs parts which you will have to buy; and it needs fuel which you will have to supply.

> **Think of your assets as fuel for your PRIM instead of money to invest.**

Most people think of their retirement assets as money they need to invest to generate income. While this is true, we'd like you to think of your assets a bit differently. In PRIM world, assets serve as fuel for your PRIM machine. This shift in thinking is a subtle but powerful reframing of how you plan and the results you will get.

In fact, we believe that overall this is a more accurate way of thinking about your investable assets. When you use your money to buy a mutual fund, annuity, or bank CD, for example, you are fueling a mini-machine which generates a certain type of outcome. For example, CDs generate interest. Stocks and mutual funds generate growth and dividends. Annuities generate lifetime income. PRIM-world thinking is seeing things for what they really are and what they really do.

You have worked hard for many years to accumulate a certain sum of money. That money must now go to work to support your lifestyle throughout retirement. The question that you must answer today is not how will you invest these funds, but what type of fuel will you use to run your PRIM?

The basic PRIM has two parts: a Guaranteed Income Driver and a Variable Income Driver.

The Basic PRIM

THE GUARANTEED INCOME DRIVER

This driver delivers **guaranteed fixed income** which sometimes rises to offset inflation. Income created by this Driver has two distinct properties that need to be considered when you build your personal PRIM. They are:

- Regular (monthly or annual) income payments that last a limited period of time.
- Regular (monthly or annual) income payments that last a lifetime.

PAYMENTS FOR A LIMITED PERIOD OF TIME

Income that comes in the form of regular payments for a **limited period of time** are typically created by mini-income machines such as:

- Certificates of Deposit
- Treasury Bonds
- Fixed-Interest Annuities
- Market-Linked CDs
- Savings Accounts
- Bonds
- Dividends
- REITs

Most of these types of mini-income machines create income in the form of interest payments and are insured by the U.S. Government, the FDIC, or an insurance company. Bonds are secured by the assets of the company issuing the bonds. Although these are not insured, if they are investment grade, they do typically provide dependable interest payments. Stocks often offer dividends, as do the interest payments from some REITS (Real Estate Investment Trusts). Neither of these, however, are insured or guaranteed.

While all these mini-income machines provide income you can count on, the income is only guaranteed at a certain rate for a limited amount of time.

For example, if you were to purchase a 5-year CD with $100,000 at 2% interest, you would receive $2,000 of annual income guaranteed for 5 years. When the guarantee period expired, the interest rate could change for the better or worse. Therefore, the income generated would also change for the better or worse. Many people who remember receiving 10 – 12% per year on bank CDs in the 80's would settle for anything above 2% today.

Another example of limited payments are REITs. These investments offered handsome yields until the 2008 market and real estate collapse. At that time many REITs defaulted on payments while others went out of business entirely (people lost their total investment). REITs can offer attractive, fixed interest payments, but there is no guarantee that they will continue in the future.

PAYMENTS FOR A LIFETIME

Income that comes in the form of regular payments for a lifetime are typically created by macro-income machines, such as:

- Social Security
- Pensions
- Annuities

These types of macro-income machines are insured by the U.S. Government, the PBGC (Pension Benefit Guarantee Corporation), or an insurance company.

This is highly dependable income that is usually guaranteed for either a single or a joint lifetime. Most people are building a pre-fueled Guaranteed Income Driver by contributing to the Social Security system. As Social Security taxes are deducted from your paychecks, you pre-purchase guaranteed regular payments of income. You are *pre-fueling* your Guaranteed Income Driver.

> You have already pre-fueled your Guaranteed Income Driver by contributing to the Social Security system.

Pensions are another pre-fueled part of the Guaranteed Income Driver. These are funded via payroll deductions or work contributions. In some cases, you might have paid nothing but have instead earned the right to a pension via your work effort over the years.

When you fuel your Guaranteed Income Driver with an income stream that is guaranteed for a lifetime (such as Social Security or a pension), we call it a *Longevity Warranty*. When you add the Longevity Warranty to your PRIM, it will look something like this:

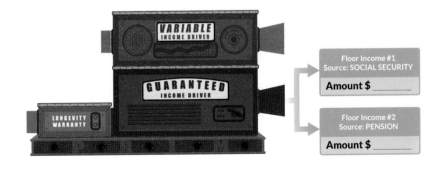

Will you need to purchase additional products to enhance your Guaranteed Income Driver? Perhaps. But the answer might be more complicated, so we'll take a closer look after we make sure you have a good understanding of your basic PRIM.

THE VARIABLE INCOME DRIVER

The Variable Income Driver is NOT compatible with the Longevity Warranty

Funds that you have invested in market-based products are all part of your Variable Income Driver. This could include your qualified retirement accounts, such as your 401(k), IRA, 403(b), SEP, and ROTH plans. It could also include your (non-qualified) brokerage or advisory accounts.

This driver generates income by selling securities when the income is needed. Because Securities have values that are susceptible to market swings, the amount of income generated and/or the amount of assets remaining will rise and fall. For these reasons, income flowing from the sale of securities via the Variable Driver is not guaranteed.

When building your personal PRIM, you will need to consider the specific qualities of the income produced from the Variable Income. These are:

- Regular (monthly or annual) income withdrawals from market based investments (typically mutual funds or ETFs) regardless of whether the market is up or down.

- Selling more shares when the market is down, and less shares when the market is up, in order to create a specific amount of income..

- Income created via the Variable Income driver is not guaranteed to last a lifetime.

DISTRIBUTIONS THAT MEET YOUR INCOME NEEDS REGARDLESS OF MARKET PERFORMANCE

Income generated from variable products is typically derived through the sale of the actual investment. These include investments in:

- Stocks
- Mutual Funds
- ETFs (Exchange Traded Funds)

For example, if you have an IRA with $100,000 invested in a mutual fund and want to generate $5,000 worth of income per year, you will need to sell some shares. If the shares are worth $12, you will need to sell 416.67 shares ($416,67 x $12 = $5,000). As the price of the mutual fund rises and falls, you will need to sell more or fewer shares to create the same $5,000.

Now your income machine would look like this:

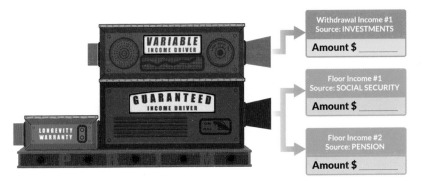

When you build your PRIM, you will determine the type of income you want, when you want it and how it will be created. When complete, your PRIM, in addition to efficiently providing you with multiple sources of income, should also give you greater confidence and peace of mind. Why? Because PRIMs are designed with your Personal Risk Style in mind, the focus of Chapter 4.

Chapter 3 Wrap-Up

☐ In the world of PRIM, investable assets serve as fuel for your income machine.

☐ The Perpetual Retirement Income Machine (PRIM) has two main parts: The Guaranteed Income Driver and the Variable Income Driver.

☐ The Guaranteed Income Driver delivers **guaranteed fixed income**.

☐ When you have an income stream that is guaranteed for life, we call it the **Longevity Warranty**.

☐ The Variable Income Driver typically generates income through the sale of shares of a security and does so regardless of market performance.

EMOTIONS DRIVE PRIM BUILDING DECISIONS

4

PRIMs are built to match your personal risk style, specifically your process of handling emotions related to risk. This is especially important when it comes to planning your money and finances. If your PRIM doesn't align with your emotional makeup, you may reach your financial goals but the journey will be one that you can't enjoy.

> "A *revolution* in the *science of emotion* has emerged in the last few decades, with the potential to create a paradigm shift in thinking about decision theories. The research reveals that emotions constitute powerful, pervasive and predictable drivers of decision making."
>
> Jennifer Lerner Harvard University
> 6.16.14

It is important that we take a close look at how your emotions react to risk. Evidence is clear that it is your emotions that drive the decisions you make. As you can see from the adjacent box, research from Harvard University has found that emotions are integral and important drivers of decision making.

WHAT IS RISK?

There is risk associated with virtually everything we do: crossing the street, investing in the stock market, walking down a flight of steps, even eating dinner if you have food allergies. In life, there is risk.

Risk comes in two broad forms:

1. **Actual Risk**

   This is risk based on the probability of an expected result occurring or not occurring based on statistical or scientific analysis.

2. Perceived Risk

This type of risk is not based on analysis or scientific evidence. It is based upon your perception of the events at hand. Usually, perceived risk is a response to a negative emotional experience that occurred in your past and is driven by those learned emotions or habits. For example, you may intellectually understand that flying is statistically one of the safest means of travel, but your perception tells you it's too dangerous or scary, so you never fly.

All risk, perceived or actual, creates a corresponding level of fear. If the level of fear is too high, you will not take the risk. However, if the level of fear is within your comfort zone, the risk becomes acceptable.

RISK IS HIGHLY PERSONAL

Because humans are all built differently, everyone has a different perception of risk and different experiences of fear associated with that risk. Look at the image below.

Corbis/Bettmann Archives

Are these men risk takers?

You would probably say yes.

However, from their point of view, they would probably say, "Not really."

Their **actual risk** is high—they are, after all, sitting 100 stories above the ground on a steel beam! However, for these men, their **perceived** *risk* is low. They understand that very few men fall, and when they do it's usually because they are careless. They have little or no fear.

Now if you were to sit on that beam with them, your **actual risk** would be the same as theirs. However, your **perceived risk** would be off the charts along with your level of fear (which is why we will never see a picture of you sitting up there having lunch with them).

The question becomes, if the evidence proves that sitting on this beam is statistically quite safe (if you are not careless), why does that data **not** outweigh your fear of falling and dying? The answer lay in the fact that our emotions are much more powerful drivers than our intellect. Decisions may be justified intellectually, but research tells us that they are powered by our emotions.

THE POWER BEHIND EMOTIONS AS DECISION MAKERS

If you look closely, you will find that risk creates all kinds of fears which you may experience as concern, frustration, worry, and stress. All these emotions are rooted in the fear that things will not go as planned and you will somehow suffer emotionally. Research is clear that as we age, our tolerance for risk goes down because the amount of fear we associate with risk goes up.

For example, many people had money in the stock market during the crash of 2008 and some (rightfully) made no changes to their portfolio. However, those nearer to retirement might have sold out of their equity positions at a loss for fear of losing more. Intellectually, they may have understood that markets go through volatile periods and always recover, but emotionally they could not handle seeing the value of their investments drop through the floor. Why?

As we age and get closer to retirement, we know that our salary from work is going to end and that our savings will have to create income for us instead. When someone close to retirement sees the value of their retirement accounts go down as they did in 2008 (some as much as 50%), emotions go through the roof. Not only are they losing money, they are losing their entire dream of retirement. Fear kicks in and they sell out at those lows, locking in losses.

> "Retirees experience *reduced risk capacity* as their lifestyle is more vulnerable to portfolio losses."
>
> Evaluating Investments versus Insurance in Retirement, June 30, 2015 Wade Pfau

Younger people, on the other hand, are still in savings or accumulation mode. They don't like losing money, but they have time to make up their losses, so they buckle up and wait it out. When recovery time is against you, losing investment value hits you financially and emotionally. This is when fear often takes over.

As you build your PRIM, always keep this in mind: when market risk is involved, some level of fear comes along for the ride. This fear comes in all shapes and sizes. Getting to know which fears impact you more than others will help you create a better PRIM.

Types of Fears Associated With Financial Risk

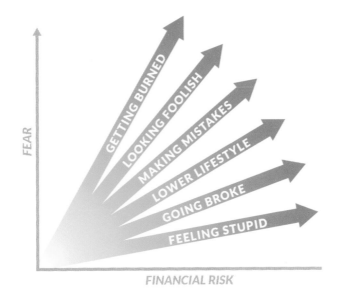

The American College of Financial Services wrote a resource document for Retirement Income Certified Professionals (RICP) that outlines eighteen risks associated with retirement. Of the eighteen, four are specifically significant to retirement income. Your level of fear for each of these risks is quite personal and depends on your risk style (how your emotions react to risk). The four retirement income risks specified by the report are:

1. **Longevity Risk**
2. **Inflation Risk**
3. **Excess Withdrawal Risk**
4. **Sequence of Return Risk**

In Chapter 5, we take a closer look at each of these Retirement Income Risks and identify how you react to them—your personal Risk Style.

Chapter 4 Wrap-Up

☐ Your PRIM will be built to reflect your Personal Risk Style.

☐ There are two kinds of risk: actual risk and perceived risk.

☐ Science shows that emotions drive decision-making, not your intellect.

☐ Fear is the root of all emotions associated with financial risk.

☐ Retirees experience reduced risk capacity as they age.

☐ There are four primary retirement income risks: Longevity, Excess Withdrawal, Inflation, and Sequence of Return risk.

CHAPTER 5

RETIREMENT INCOME RISKS AND YOUR PERSONAL RISK STYLE

5

In this chapter, we are going to take a deep dive into understanding each of the retirement income risks, assess your emotional reaction to them, and then determine your Personal Risk Style. This will help you build a PRIM that is both financially fulfilling and emotionally comfortable throughout your retirement journey.

LONGEVITY RISK

> "The 85-and-over United States population, the fastest-growing cohort in the country ..."
>
> Older Americans Key Indicators of Well-Being — Federal Interagency Forum on Aging 2016

Longevity Risk creates the fear of outliving your income.

Living beyond your income can have severely adverse effects on your lifestyle, sense of independence, and emotions. It could mean having to live with your children, being supported by the government or outright homelessness. The loss of independence can be quite embarrassing and emotionally difficult to acknowledge.

We all know that people are living longer. Back in the 1950s for example, people did not need much retirement planning. During those years, when someone retired at age 65, their expected lifespan was only another seven years or so. It's not terribly difficult to plan for just seven years in the future, and most people simply made-do. In the 1950s there was little fear about outliving your income.

The retirement planning picture today is quite different. A person retiring at 65 is expected to live well into their 80's, and possibly longer.

The fastest growing population in America is people living beyond age 90. If that turns out to be you, a retirement of 25 to 30 years is not out of the question.

Under the best of circumstances, managing retirement income for that long is quite challenging. In fact, 41% of CPA financial planners say running out of money is their clients' top concern, including clients who have a high net worth.

> "Forty-one percent of CPA financial planners say running out of money is their clients' top concern about retirement— including those who have a high net worth."

And it doesn't end there.

Further research reveals that 61% of people between the ages of 44 to 75 fear running out of money more than they fear death.

Which Do You Fear More?
Age 44 – 75

39%
Fear of Death

61%
Fear of Running Out of Money

Source: Allianz Life Insurance

What does this all mean? Almost everyone is subject to *Longevity Risk*.

Now it's your turn.

Take a moment and ask yourself what your life would be like if you prematurely spent-down your money and saw your income disappear while you were still quite healthy.

How would you feel if you lost your independence? What if you had to rely on family, friends, or the government for assistance? What if you had no choice but to cut back on all the things you enjoy, like travel, restaurants, movies, and music?

How you answer these questions will give you an idea of the level of fear you attach to this retirement issue. On a scale of 1 – 5, where 1 means you have absolutely no fear attached to this issue and 5 means that it is off the charts, where would you put yourself?

My Longevity Fear Ranking:

INFLATION RISK

Inflation Risk results in the fear of loss of lifestyle (quality of life) because your income will not keep up with increases in the cost of living. When income falls behind the rate of inflation, the amount you can buy for each dollar goes down leaving you with two choices:

1. Cut back on your expenditures, which means your standard of living goes down.

2. Deplete your savings to make up the loss of purchasing power, which then opens the door to another risk: Excess Withdrawal Risk (discussed next).

How Inflation Affects Purchasing Power

Inflation risk is slow moving. It eats away, little by little, year after year, at the value of your money. Many people hardly notice, until one day they wake up and realize they can't afford to buy the same items because things have become so much more expensive.

Let's look at this another way. If an item costs $1 today, it would cost $1.05 after one year of 5% inflation. However, after ten years of 5% inflation that same $1 item would cost nearly $1.63 due to compounding.

The chart below shows what things could cost in the future:

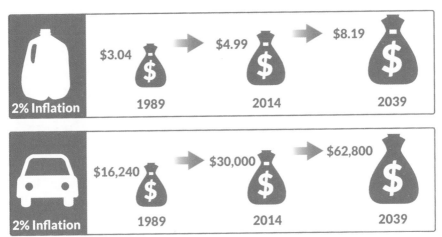

2% Inflation — $3.04 — 1989 → $4.99 — 2014 → $8.19 — 2039

2% Inflation — $16,240 — 1989 → $30,000 — 2014 → $62,800 — 2039

Fidelity Investments - Fundamentals of Retirement Income Planning

Most people are concerned about inflation, but rarely do they describe it as 'fear', the way they would describe running out of money or experiencing a potential stock market collapse. Nevertheless, inflation's long-term effects can be devastating.

Okay, now it's your turn again.

Take a moment and ask yourself what life would be like if your income did not rise to offset inflation.

Would you be concerned if you found yourself unable to afford the things you enjoy? Would you feel pressure or anxiety every time you went to the store? Would you make substitutions and buy cheaper versions of things you like?

On a scale of 1 – 5, where 1 means you have absolutely no fear attached to this issue and 5 means that it is off the charts, where would you put yourself?

My Inflation Fear Ranking:

EXCESS WITHDRAWAL RISK

Excess Withdrawal Risk results in the fear of running out of money as assets deplete at a much higher rate than planned. When people do run out of money during retirement, it is not uncommon for them to suffer emotionally as they lose their identity, sense of well-being and sense of independence. Add to that embarrassment and the stress of being forced into difficult choices for self and family, it is no wonder that the fear associated with this risk comes as no surprise.

Imagine this: you and your partner are stranded on a desert island with a bottle of water and two cups. You stumble on a magic lantern during your search for food. Upon rubbing the magic lantern, a genie appears! He tells you that he will come on a regular schedule to refill your water bottle, however he has certain rules:

1. You drink two cups of water a day, enough to sustain yourselves comfortably.

2. He will only add two cups of water to your supply each time he comes.

3. If there is no more water in the bottle he will not add any water at all.

4. If you want, you may drink more than two cups of water, but if the bottle is empty, he will no longer come.

You and your partner follow the genie's directions and drink only two cups of water a day. You find that you live well and the genie appears every day to refill the two cups of water. Life is good and you always have a full bottle of water.

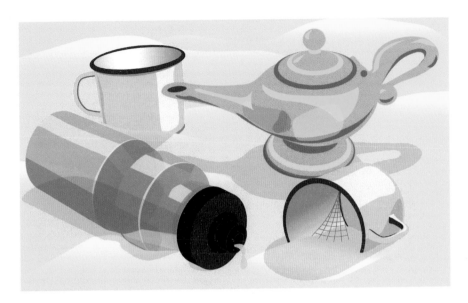

Soon, however, a rare heat wave arrives at the island and it gets much hotter than you can bear. The heat is so unbearable your heads throb and sweat begins to pour out of each of you like an open faucet. As your thirst goes through the roof, you realize that you can no longer sustain yourselves sharing two cups of water. You need to drink more to survive, and you do. Now, every time the Genie appears, despite the refill, you see the level of water in the bottle slowly diminishing.

Then one day your partner falls ill and his temperature skyrockets. He needs to drink even more water to hydrate and to keep the fever down. Without realizing it, and with no other choice, you give your partner the last drops of water from the bottle. Then it hits you both—no more water. And, no more Genie!

Imagine if that were you and your loved one on the island. How would you feel at the moment of realization that things are not going to work out too well for you? It would probably be devastating, wouldn't it?

Excess withdrawal risk works the same way as our desert friends' water. In a perfect world, each time you withdraw funds from your investments for income, your money will replenish itself and grow back to its original level.

Unfortunately, if you begin taking larger withdrawals due to inflation or an emergency, your money will not have the time necessary to fully replenish. Like the bottle of water in the desert, your money will eventually run dry. When that happens, your income (your two cups of water) will run dry as well.

Excess withdrawals can hide under your financial radar, until one day you wake up and realize you are about to run out of money. By then, of course, it's too late to fix the problem. Running out of money due to excess withdrawals from your investments will not end as badly as the story, but it will change your life, always for the worse.

In the illustration below, look at how quickly assets deplete as the withdrawal percentage increases.

Excess Withdrawal and Rates of Asset Depletion

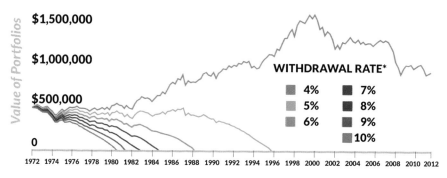

*Hypothetical value of assets held in a tax-deferred account after adjusting for monthly withdrawals and performance. Initial investment of $500,000 invested in a portfolio of 50% stocks, 40% bonds, and 10% short-term investments. Hypothetical illustration uses historical monthly performance from January 1972 through December 2011 from Ibbotson Associates: stocks, bonds, and short-term investments are represented by the S&P 500® Index, U.S. intermediate-term government bond, and U.S. 30-day T-Bills, respectively. Initial withdrawal amount based on 1/12th of applicable withdrawal rate multiplied by $500,000. Subsequent withdrawal amounts based on prior month's amount adjusted by the actual monthly change in the Consumer Price Index for that month. This chart is for illustrative purposes only and is not indicative of any investment. Past performance is no guarantee of future results. Important Information and Methodology can be found at end of presentation.   Fidelity Investments - Fundamentals of Retirement Planning

Again, it's your turn.

Take a moment and ask yourself what your life would be like if you began taking excess withdrawals and saw the level of your assets dropping month after month.

Would you continue to live life as normal? Would you be nervous watching your assets deplete faster than expected? Would the prospect of running out of money put stress and pressure on you and your loved ones?

On a scale of 1 – 5, where 1 means you have absolutely no fear attached to this issue and 5 means that it is off the charts, where would you put yourself?

My Excess Withdrawal Fear Ranking:

SEQUENCE OF RETURN RISK

Most people understand **Market Risk**; the fear of losing money when the stock market declines. However, few people understand **Sequence of Return Risk**; the risk of taking systematic withdrawals from investments when the market is declining. Taking withdrawals by selling assets when the market is falling is a bad idea in most circumstances because:

1. You are compounding a loss by selling shares when the market is low.

2. When the market recovers, you have less assets available to take advantage of the recovery.

Taking withdrawals by selling assets when the market is falling at the beginning of your retirement years (the sequence of negative returns is working against you) is an especially bad idea. Why? Research shows the likelihood of an early depletion of savings rises dramatically.

Let's say you retire at age 65 and start taking withdrawals from your market-based 401(K) to produce retirement income. If the market goes up 5%, and you

> "... If a retiree is unfortunate enough to be exposed to a *sequence of adverse returns early in retirement,* the likelihood of an early *depletion of savings* rises dramatically."
>
> W. Van Harlow, PhD, CFA Director of Research at The Putnam Institute

then withdraw only the gains, your principal remains intact.

However, if the market goes down 5%, not only have you lost principal, but you still must make a withdrawal for your needed income. This further compounds your losses by forcing you to take out *additional* principal. The market did not provide a good "sequence" of return for you.

Below is a comparison of how positive and negative sequence of returns can affect retirees. In the example, both investors begin with the same asset value: $250,000. They experience the same average growth rate of 6.6% over a 30-year period. As a matter of fact, they have the exact same returns, just in *reverse* order. They also withdraw the same amount of money each year ($12,500 inflated by 3% for inflation).

Investor A experiences an unfortunate *sequence of returns* in the first three years by enduring negative market returns. Investor B experiences the same losses, but not until the last three years (a fortunate sequence). As you can see, Investor A runs out of money by year 17; Investor B still has assets remaining after 31 years.

Return Sequencing Results (Success or Failure)

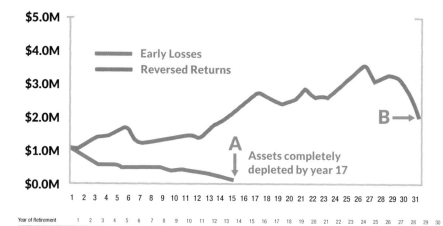

Year of Retirement	1	2	3	4	5	6	7	8	9	10	11	12	13	14	15	16	17	18	19	20	21	22	23	24	25	26	27	28	29	30
Losses Early Returns (0%)	-17.5	-11.3	-4.6	-9.6	-9.8	12.1	13.1	18.4	6.0	-8.3	18.4	7.2	-3.7	-1.0	13.0	16.9	23.6	15.9	25.6	-0.3	9.9	8.6	16.2	-1.8	-19.7	14.1	6.6	17.6	25.9	9.9
Losses Early Returns (0%)	9.9	25.9	17.6	6.6	14.1	-19.7	-1.8	16.2	8.6	9.9	-0.3	25.6	15.9	23.6	16.9	13.0	-1.0	-3.7	7.2	18.4	-8.3	6.0	18.4	13.1	12.1	-9.8	9.6	-4.6	-11.3	-17.5

Sequence of returns can be a true ally, or it can be the reason your income fails you in retirement. The problem, of course, is that no one can predict when the market will decide to tumble! This is why building a PRIM using only a market-based Variable Income Driver is not for the faint-hearted.

Your turn again.

Take a moment and ask yourself how you would feel if you experienced both market losses and an adverse sequence of returns early in retirement.

Would you feel comfortable taking a withdrawal out of a depreciating asset? Would you have confidence that your portfolio would bounce back? Could you sleep at night if you were making withdrawals and experienced another market decline like we did in 2008?

On a scale of 1 – 5, where 1 means you have absolutely no fear attached to this issue and 5 means that it is off the charts, where would you put yourself?

My Sequence of Return Fear Ranking:

Your PRIM will be designed to provide a lasting and steady flow of increasing income during your retirement. However, the end-goal is more emotional than financial. It needs to give you the confidence and peace of mind about the future. If your PRIM is built out-of-sync with your risk style, it is very likely that you will suffer emotionally.

Each of the retirement income risks plays its part in making your life feel like an emotional roller coaster, a still lake, or somewhere in between. Some fears will be more prominent than others; some will cause immediate anxiety; and others will fester over longer periods of time. When looked at as a whole, however, these individual fears combine to determine your Personal Risk Style. Score yourself on the following chart and then identify your Risk Style.

IDENTIFYING YOUR RISK STYLE

Now let's add up your fear rankings and identify your risk style:

Longevity Fear Ranking

Inflation Fear Ranking

Excess Withdrawal Fear Ranking

Sequence of Return Fear Ranking

TOTAL

Compare your total fear score with the key below to determine your risk style:

Score 4 – 8   **You are a:**   RISK TAKER

You have ice in your veins, and risk doesn't seem to have much of an emotional effect on you.

Score 16 – 20   **You are a:**   RISK AVOIDER

Risk is not your cup of tea. If you see risk coming, you prefer to move in another direction.

Score 9 – 15   **You are a:**   RISK MANAGER

You are willing to take managed risk but are careful about it.

Do you agree with the evaluation? Here's another way to check the results.

Imagine here you are walking on a mountain path and suddenly you come to wide crevasse. You must get to the other side. Look at each of the pictures below. Without trying to think it through, select the one that you are immediately drawn to—do you jump over; turn around to find another way; or build a bridge?

A.

RISK TAKER

Risk Takers embrace risk. The upside potential and the excitement that risk brings with it all serve to outweigh any fear of danger or loss. If they fall, it's no problem. They just pull themselves up and try again. These risk takers like to wing it and sometimes the ride is more important than the results.

B.

RISK AVOIDER

Risk Avoiders march to a different beat. These types simply do not like the downside. They fear making mistakes that may hurt them in the future. Risk stresses them out.

C.

RISK MANAGER

Risk Managers figure out how to take measured risk. This may be uncomfortable for them, but they understand it may be in their best interests. Balance is the keyword for risk managers.

Each PRIM uses a specific technique by which its drivers produce income.

- **Risk Takers** use some type of Systematic Withdrawal technique such as a percentage of assets.

- **Risk Avoiders** use a Flooring approach which guarantees a floor of income to assure that certain expenses are always covered.

- **Risk Managers** use a Bucket System and employ a combination of techniques whereby each bucket creates income for specific periods of time as you age.

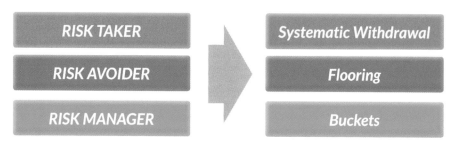

Each technique works differently and each has its pros and cons. In the following chapter we'll explore each technique and explain why each caters to a specific Risk Syle.

Chapter 5 Wrap-Up

- ☐ Longevity Risk raises the fear of outliving income.
- ☐ People fear running out of income more than they fear death.
- ☐ Inflation Risk raises the fear that your income does not keep up with the rise of prices over time.
- ☐ Excess Withdrawal Risk raises the fear of depleting assets too quickly.
- ☐ Sequence of Return Risk results when the market has negative returns early in a person's withdrawal period and thereby raises the fear of accelerated asset depletion.
- ☐ If your PRIM is built out-of-sync with your Risk Style, you will suffer emotionally.
- ☐ The 3 risk styles are Risk Taker, Risk Avoider, and Risk Manager.

CHAPTER 6

THE
RISK TAKER'S
PRIM

6

The Risk Taker's PRIM puts heavy emphasis on the Variable Income Driver. Risk Taker's, however, still use the Fixed Income Driver for income that has already been pre-fueled during their working years, i.e. Social Security and pensions.

The Variable Income Driver, because it is dependent on the unpredictable movement of the markets, provides income that is neither fixed nor guaranteed for any period of time. The potentials for higher gains, higher income, and possibly a higher lifestyle are what draw in the Risk Taker.

In its simplest form, the Risk Taker's PRIM would look like this:

MEET MAGGIE AND STAN

Maggie and Stan are planning their retirement income. They have worked hard over the years and have diligently saved in their 401(k)s and IRAs. They put two children through college, and like most couples, have had their financial ups and downs. Now they are looking forward to what they consider to be a very special time in their life: retirement. They don't want to kick back and become couch potatoes. Instead, they plan to move forward and grow in ways that were not open to them during their working years.

Here's an overview of their situation:

Maggie and Stan's Financial Overview	Comments
Total Investable Assets	$1,000,000
Total Desired Retirement Income	$85,000 Gross Before Taxes
Age	Both are 66
Social Security	$35,000 Annually for Both
Pension	$10,000 Annually for Both no COLA*
Risk Style	Risk Takers

* COLA – Cost of Lifing Adjustment

A SIDE NOTE ABOUT PENSIONS:

We are assuming that Maggie and Stan have a pension. For many Americans, pensions are a disappearing source of income. Years ago, it was common for people to work for one company a long time and that company would provide a pension when they retired. Over time, pensions have been replaced by 401(k)s. Many companies choose to provide matching contributions to the 401(k) instead of providing an expensive pension. In doing so, research shows that investment risk has been transferred from the company to the individual.

"The result was an acceleration of America's *shift away* from defined-benefit (DB) pensions toward defined-contribution (DC) retirement plans, *which transfers the investment risk* from the company to the employee."

The Crisis in Retirement Planning by Robert C. Merton, The Harvard Business Review

So, if you have a pension, feel fortunate that the company is continuing to bear the investment risk in addition to other risks such as **Longevity**, **Withdrawal**, **Cognitive Risk** (losing the ability to think and make decisions), and **Rules & Regulation Risk** (changes in government rules and regulation which could cause a business to lose sales and profits).

Back to Maggie and Stan.

Their first job is to figure out whether they have an income overage or shortfall. To find out, they add their Social Security and pensions to determine their guaranteed sources of income ($45,000). Then they subtract that total from their desired income of $85,000, resulting in an income shortfall of $40,000, the gross amount of income they need to generate from their PRIM before taxes.

> **NOTE:** To keep things simple and stay focused on the concepts rather than specific numbers, we are going to use gross income before taxes in all our examples.

Maggie and Stan's Income Shortfall Calculation	Amount
Total Income Needed	$85,000
Current Guaranteed Income Social Security	$35,000 – Combined
Current Guaranteed Income Pension	$10,000 – Combined
Total All Current Guaranteed Income	$45,000
Income Shortfall	-$40,000

In this example, Maggie and Stan are Risk Takers. They believe that if they can get great results investing in the stock market, they will be able to generate more income and live a better lifestyle. Therefore, their Variable Income Driver will be fueled to generate the $40,000 income shortfall.

FUELING THE VARIABLE INCOME DRIVER

Variable Income Drivers produce income through a Systematic Withdrawal Strategy, at a rate often called the Safe Money Withdrawal Rate

(SMW). Historically, the most popular SMW rate was 4%, commonly called the 4% Rule. This rate was determined back in the early 1990s by a financial planner named William (Bill) Bengen. Bengen tested several retirement withdrawal rates over long periods of time and determined that a retiree with a balanced (50/50) portfolio split between large-cap stocks and intermediate-term U.S. bonds, should be able to withdraw 4% of the original account balance in the first year of retirement. Each withdrawal after the first one would include the original withdrawal amount and an adjustment upwards to offset inflation. His method sought to give the retiree a 30-year period of not running out of money.

In the case of Maggie and Stan, they would withdraw $40,000 (4%) of their investable assets ($1,000,000) in year one. Then, no matter how their portfolio performed, they would withdraw another $40,000 in year two, adjusted for inflation, which would be $41,200. In year three they would withdraw $42,436 and so on. This way, they would always maintain their purchasing power.

Bengen's 4% Rule has become a cornerstone of retirement income planning. Michael Herndon, Vice-President for Financial Resilience at AARP said, "It's like eating four vegetables a day!" It's one of those rules that is so common that most advisers and retirees never questioned its validity—until recently.

> "... you should probably stick to a 3% rate."
>
> Retirement Rules: Rethinking a 4% Withdrawal Rate, Wade Pfau, Barrons

Recent research, however, challenges the 4% Rule. Higher levels of market volatility, increasing life-spans, historically low interest rates, increasing health care expenses, and concern about sequence of returns risk have transformed this rule into something new:

Although a 3% withdrawal rate is now recommended, many retirees (and advisors) still use the 4% number. Therefore, we will illustrate the Variable Income Driver with the 4% withdrawal rate.

The Risk Taker's PRIM Utilizing a 4% SMW Rate

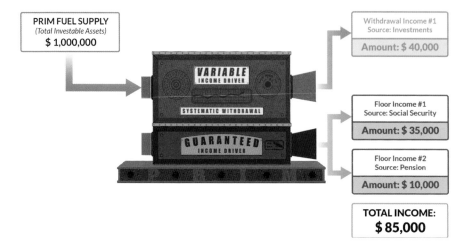

Notice a few things here:

- With the PRIM, assets are thought of in terms of fuel rather than money that needs to be invested. This allows one to be more objective and less emotional about specific investment choices.

- Money is invested in a diversified portfolio of stocks and bonds per the Bengen rule (50/50).

- The Guaranteed Income Driver will produce income from Social Security and a pension which has already been pre-fueled.

UP MARKET SCENARIO

When the market is rising, the 4% Rule works quite well. It preserves and grows assets while providing the initial income level, plus the withdrawals increase each year for an estimated inflation rate of 3%.

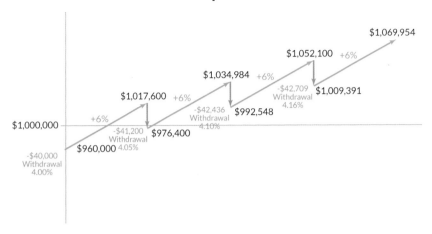

Systematic Withdrawal Results in an Up Market

This is great news for Maggie and Stan. Not only is their income goal met, but their assets will continue to grow. Additionally, all the retirement income risks are covered:

- Longevity Risk — their income will last as long as they do.

- Excess Withdrawal Risk — they can afford to take out more if needed.

- Inflation Risk — income is adjusted every year to keep up with cost of living.

- Sequence of Return Risk — there is no problem, the market is rising.

DOWN MARKET SCENARIO

Of course, there are two sides to every story. So, now let's look at what happens when the market is falling. As you can see, Maggie and Stan have a very different experience from that of a rising market. Unfortunately, this is going to test their risk fortitude, because they will see their savings quickly diminish before their eyes.

Systematic Withdrawal Results in a Down Market

$1,000,000

-$40,000
Withdrawal
4.00%

$960,000

-6%

$902,400

$861,200

-$41,200
Withdrawal
4.57%

-6%

$809,528

$767,092

-$42,436
Withdrawal
5.24%

-6%

$721,066

$678,357

-$42,709
Withdrawal
5.92%

-6%

$637,656

While Maggie and Stan still receive their inflation adjusted income each year, their overall financial situation unravels at an accelerated rate. In a down market (a poor sequence of returns), the Variable Income Driver will need to take an increased percentage of the asset each year. As you can see in the above diagram, the starting withdrawal rate is 4%. Each year that withdrawal rate has to rise to reach the dollar figure desired. After just three years, it has risen to almost 6%. In another few years the withdrawal rate will be over 10%. At these increased withdrawal rates, it is obvious Maggie and Stan will quickly run out of money.

There's no good news for Maggie and Stan. In this scenario, all the retirement income risks are in play:

- Longevity Risk — when they run out of money, income stops, yet they could easily live for many more years.

- Excess Withdrawal Risk — a larger percentage must be withdrawn each year, compounding losses and accelerating their journey to zero.

- Inflation Risk — initially this is covered due to increased withdrawals, however, this risk comes fully into play once the portfolio is diminished.

- Sequence of Return Risk — the sequence is working against them and when the market recovers, they will have less assets in play with which to recoup their losses.

THE UNCERTAINTY ZONE

Let's compare the up and down market scenarios on the same chart:

Risk Taker's Market Comparison: Up vs Down Scenarios

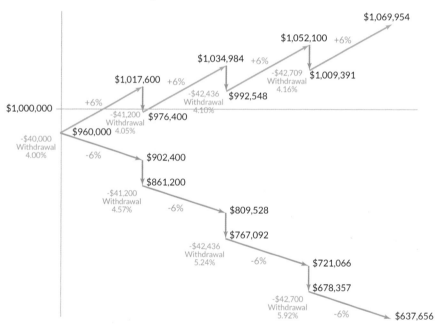

Clearly, there are very different results depending on market conditions (positive vs negative sequence of returns). However, markets rarely go straight up or straight down for long periods of time. Instead, they are variable and volatile. Therefore, predicting results becomes increasingly difficult.

If Maggie and Stan think of the scenarios presented here as best and worst case scenarios, then the area in between is known as the **Uncertainty Zone** (for the value of the remaining assets).

Risk Taker's Uncertainty Zone

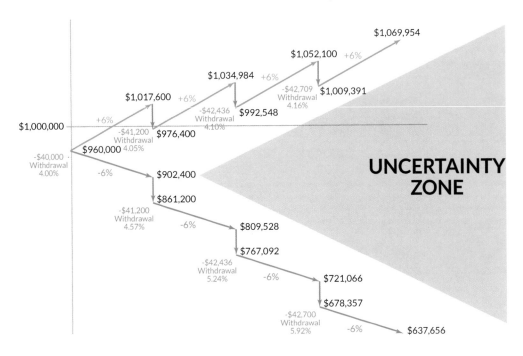

The *Uncertainty Zone* is the level of uncertainty that exists between the best and worse case scenarios.

The Uncertainty Zone gets wider and larger the further out in time you go. It is this Uncertainty Zone (for remaining asset value) that a Risk Taker can tolerate in exchange for a potentially higher lifestyle throughout retirement.

THE PROS AND CONS OF
THE SYSTEMATIC WITHDRAWAL APPROACH

What Retirement Researcher Wade Pfau* says about this approach:

The Pros of this approach:

- The potential for a better lifestyle throughout retirement.

- Should decent market returns materialize, investment solutions can be sustained over a long retirement.

- Portfolio balances are liquid in the sense that they are fully accessible and not part of a contractual agreement.

- The potential to generate upside growth from investments can support a larger legacy.

The Cons of this approach:

- The dual impact of sequence & longevity risk threatens the ability to support a desired lifestyle.

- Retirees experience reduced risk capacity as their lifestyle is more vulnerable to portfolio losses.

- One must plan for how declining cognitive abilities will hamper the ability to manage investments.

- Efforts to plan for a long life also require a lower spending rate.

- Longevity protection is not guaranteed.

- Assets are less liquid than they appear if they are spent too early and if needs later in life can no longer be met.

- Downside risk could materialize, leading to asset depletion and the possibility of a "reverse legacy" as relatives are called upon to provide support.

* Quoted from, Evaluating Investments versus Insurance in Retirement, June 30, 2015 Wade Pfau

Chapter 6 Wrap-Up

- [ ] Risk Takers will build their PRIM with heavy emphasis on the Variable Income Driver and a goal of a potentially higher lifestyle.

- [ ] The Guaranteed Income Driver is only used for Social Security and pensions that have been pre-fueled.

- [ ] Systematic withdrawals are used to create income.

- [ ] The Safe Money Withdrawal Rate allows for an initial 4% withdrawal of invested assets, adjusted for annual inflation.

- [ ] New research suggests you should stick to a 3% Safe Money Withdrawal Rate.

- [ ] The Systematic Withdrawal approach works very well in an up market, avoiding the most detrimental aspects of the four retirement income risks.

- [ ] In down markets this strategy falls short, exacerbating all the retirement income risks.

- [ ] The Uncertainty Zone is the area that exists between the best and worst case scenarios.

- [ ] The Uncertainty Zone resulting from Systematic Withdrawals and Market Volatility is bigger and wider than other approaches.

CHAPTER 7

THE
RISK AVOIDER'S
PRIM

7

The Risk Avoider's PRIM concentrates heavily on the certainty of income produced by the Guaranteed Income Driver. This driver provides income that is fixed and guaranteed because it is programmed to use financial products that offer this type of surety.

License to Spend: a feeling of greater entitlement to spend as their worry about future income is lower.

License to Spend: Consumption-Income Sensitivity and Portfolio Choice • Jawad M. Addoum Stefanos Delikouras George M. Korniotis November 13, 2014 Abstract

When income is highly predictable, it adds to a person's ability to enjoy that income by giving them a psychological "license to spend."

The Risk Avoider's PRIM would look like this in its simplest form:

The Risk Avoider's PRIM

FUELING THE RISK AVOIDER'S PRIM

Risk Avoiders use a *flooring* strategy to get predictable, safe income.

RISK AVOIDER → *Flooring*

Flooring is a strategy where you set a **baseline income** goal that needs to be guaranteed under all circumstances. For many, baseline income is defined as your baseline living expenses. This becomes the floor of your PRIM.

Let's say that Maggie and Stan have morphed into Risk Avoiders. They still want $40,000 of additional income over their Social Security and pension (for a total of $85,000), but they need it guaranteed, because it is their baseline minimum to maintain their lifestyle. To achieve this goal, they will fuel their Guaranteed Income Driver using a fixed annuity which creates $40,0000 per year.

Given their ages (each 66), they will need to put about $727,272 into a fixed annuity. The remaining $272,728 will be placed in savings and used for emergencies, luxury purchases, and to offset future cost-of-living increases. It could also be placed in an annuity designed for growth rather than income if it wasn't needed for other purposes.

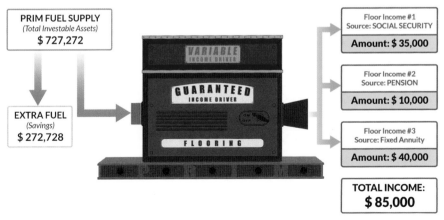

It is important to note here that Maggie and Stan could have chosen to use their entire fuel supply ($1,000,000) to power their Guaranteed Income Driver. If they did, they would receive payments of $55,000 annually, instead of the $40,000 needed to fulfill their plan (in Chapter 6 we'll show you how to make these annuity payout calculations). If there are more than sufficient assets to create the Floor, as is the case with Maggie and Stan, it becomes a personal decision as to how to invest the overage.

> **NOTE:** In this example and in the illustrations to follow we have placed 100% of Maggie and Stan's assets into fixed annuity products. We've done so just for illustration purposes. In real life you would rarely, if ever, put 100% of your assets into a annuity product.

WHY THE GUARANTEED INCOME DRIVER MUST USE ANNUITIES

Maggie and Stan want their income payments guaranteed for the rest of their life. To accomplish this, they must use annuities. Annuities are the only products that guarantee lifetime income. When an annuity is used for income, Longevity Risk is shifted from the performance of the market to the guarantee of an insurance company.

The word "annuity" simply means a sum of money that is paid regularly. Fixed annuities, guaranteed by insurance companies, have an impeccable history of safety. A specific annuity appropriate for Maggie and Stan is called the Fixed Index Annuity (FIA). This type allows Maggie and Stan to participate in the growth of the market when it rises (subject to a cap), but they suffer no losses when the market declines. More importantly, this type of annuity offers an **Income Rider** used to generate guaranteed lifetime income.

> The word *annuity* simply means a sum of money that is paid regularly.

It's important to bring up an important distinction in terminology here, because sometimes *Income Rider* and traditional *Annuitization* are confused. When an annuity is **Annuitized**, your assets are transferred to the insurance company who then guarantees income for the rest of your life. In other words, you lose control of the assets. When an *Income Rider** is used, your assets remain in your control. This gives you flexibility, a death benefit, preservation of your assets, and continued growth during the distribution phase.

> When an *Income Rider* is used, your assets remain in your control. This gives you flexibility, a death benefit, preservation of your assets, and continued growth during the distribution phase.

While it's not the scope of this book to go into details about specific products and how they work, use this checklist to make sure your annuity has the following features:

FIXED INDEX ANNUITY CHECKLIST

Income is the result of employing an Income Rider, not annuitizing

Make sure it's a Fixed Annuity and that there is no Market Risk

It has an option for income to increase during distribution to offset inflation (rising income option)

The Account Value has the ability to grow while you are receiving income during the distribution phase

It is flexible, allowing annual penalty-free withdrawals and other withdrawals under special circumstances i.e. nursing home

There are no or low annual fees

It must have a Death Benefit whereby proceeds go to a beneficiary, not the insurance company

The surrender period is 10 years or less

*Income Riders are often optional at an additional cost.

UP MARKET SCENARIO

When the stock market is rising, all solutions do well, including the *Flooring* approach. However, Fixed Index Annuities (FIA) have limits on what they can earn each year. These are called caps or participation rates.

For example, let's say the S&P 500 Index rises 10% and the annuity has a cap of a 4% increase. The annuity will be credited with 4% interest which is locked in. Then, let's say the index falls 20% the next year. The annuity will not lose anything (because it is a fixed product), therefore it will be credited with 0% for the year.

Cap rates currently range from 3.5% – 6.5%. Some annuities have no caps, but in those cases, they have other factors built into them whereby they can earn a higher rate, but still less than that of the market.

In this example, we assume that the market is rising at 6% annually, but the annuity earns 4% per year interest due to its 4% cap. During this time, Maggie and Stan are generating $40,000 per year of income which the annuity guarantees. We also assume that the remaining Savings is also deposited in a Fixed Annuity that earns 4% per year but does not produce any additional income (although that is an option for Maggie and Stan if they wanted more income).

Flooring Approach — Up Market Scenario

Let's now compare the results of the Risk Avoider to the Risk Taker. As you can see, even though the Risk Avoider takes far less risk than the Risk Taker, the results, because no money is lost when the market declines, are still fairly close.

| Systematic Withdrawal | $1,068,894 |
| Flooring | $989,195 |

The combination of growth (albeit limited) with no market losses results in a balance of assets that remain stable. The addition of a lifetime of guaranteed income assures Maggie and Stan they will never run out of a paycheck and will probably have money left over for a legacy, another benefit of using the right type of fixed annuity. In our example, if there was a death after the fourth year, $957,200 would be paid to beneficiaries ($674,763 + $282,437), and would be done so free of probate, public notice and other delays.

Back to the up-market scenario:

This is a good situation for our Risk Avoiders. Their income goal is met for life, and they have growth opportunities (though limited) on their remaining assets. However, not all the Retirement Income Risks are covered:

- Longevity Risk — their income will last as long as they do.

- Excess Withdrawal Risk — they can afford to take out more if needed from their extra fuel (savings).

- Inflation Risk — income, in this scenario, does **not** rise every year to keep up with the cost of living.

- Sequence of Return Risk — nothing is invested in the market, so there is no Sequence of Return Risk

DOWN MARKET SCENARIO

The *Flooring* approach works especially well in a down market scenario:

Flooring Approach — Down Market Scenario

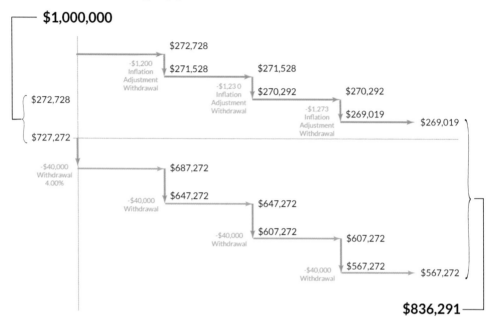

When markets fall, fixed annuities suffer no losses. Therefore, shares are never sold at lower prices to create income. The withdrawal is simply deducted from principal. In other words, fixed annuities provide guaranteed income, but since they are not market-based products, they do not compound a loss by selling shares when prices are low.

The account value of the fixed annuity decreases only when there is a withdrawal. At some point, despite the fact that the account value does not lose value when there are losses, withdrawals for income could deplete the account value to zero. If, however, the withdrawals are the result of an Income Rider, if the account value does reach zero, the Income Rider guarantees that income will continue for your lifetime.

Now let's compare the results of the down market scenarios for the Risk Taker and the Risk Avoider. As you can see, the Flooring approach preserves assets better in a down market than the Systematic Withdrawal approach.

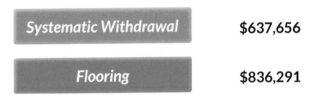

| Systematic Withdrawal | $637,656 |
| Flooring | $836,291 |

Looking at the four retirement income risks during a down market, they have not changed when compared with the up market:

- Longevity Risk – income will last as long as they do.
- Excess Withdrawal Risk – they can afford to take out more if needed from their extra fuel (savings).
- Inflation Risk – income, in this scenario, does not rise every year to keep up with cost of living.
- Sequence of Return Risk – nothing is invested in the market, so there is no Sequence of Return Risk.

The Flooring Approach Comparison

Once again Maggie and Stan can think of the scenarios presented here as best case and worst case scenarios, with the area in between defined as the uncertainty zone.

Risk Avoider's Uncertainty Zone

When we put the Risk Avoider's and the Risk Taker's uncertainty zones on the same diagram, it is easy to see that the difference is extensive.

Risk Avoider vs Risk Taker's Uncertainty Zones

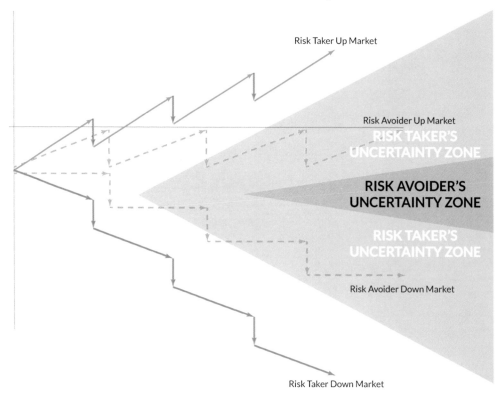

ADDING THE LONGEVITY WARRANTY & SEQUENCE OF RETURN BUFFER

The guaranteed income for life offered by the annuity allows Maggie and Stan to cross Longevity Risk off their worries list. They can now label a new part of their PRIM: *The Longevity Warranty.*

Additionally, they have avoided the dangers of Sequence of Return Risk by staying out of the market and utilizing a fixed annuity, which means they can add another part to their PRIM: *The Sequence of Return Buffer.* With these added parts, Maggie and Stan's PRIM has evolved into a nifty income machine:

The Flooring Approach With Longevity Warranty & Sequence of Return Buffer

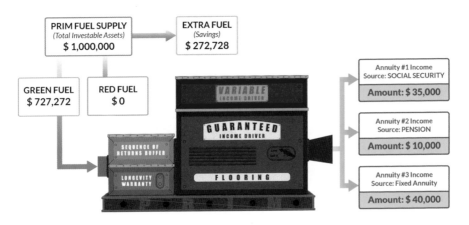

Okay. But what about inflation? They have extra money in savings that can be used to offset inflation, but that may not be a long-term solution. Inflation is more difficult to solve using only the flooring approach. However, the solution is found by combining two approaches which we outline in the next chapter.

THE PROS AND CONS OF THE FLOORING APPROACH

What Retirement Researcher Wade Pfau* says about this approach:

The Pros of this approach:

- Guarantees provide peace of mind and a license to spend, which leads to a less stressful and more enjoyable retirement experience.
- Income is guaranteed for life.
- Some solutions can provide liquidity at a cost.
- A fixed annuity providing a lifetime of income dedicates assets toward that need, allowing other assets to be earmarked for growth.
- With more income from mortality credits (where premiums paid by those who die earlier than expected contribute to gains of the overall pool) over long retirements, it eventually supports a larger total legacy.

The Cons of this approach:

- Fixed annuities have limited upside potential.
- Concern with the ability of insurance companies to meet contractual guarantees over the long term.
- Additional costs for liquidity may be high.
- Legacy benefits are not offered without additional riders, which reduce the availability of mortality credits (where premiums paid by those who die earlier than expected contribute to gains of the overall pool).

* Quoted from, Evaluating Investments versus Insurance in Retirement, June 30, 2015 Wade Pfau'

Chapter 7 Wrap-Up

☐ Risk Avoiders will build their PRIM focusing solely on using the Guaranteed Income Driver.

☐ The *Flooring* approach is used to guarantee a baseline minimum income.

☐ Fixed annuities with *Income Riders* are used to guarantee the *Income Floor.*

☐ Less assets may be required to produce the income needed, leaving money over which may be place in savings or a growth focused fixed annuity.

☐ The *Flooring* approach works well in an up market, but does not grow as well as the *Systematic Withdrawal* strategy.

☐ In down markets, this strategy effectively protects baseline income.

☐ The flooring approach has a narrower band of *uncertainty*.

CHAPTER 8

THE RISK MANAGER'S PRIM

PRIM building for Risk Managers requires that they use a ***measured risk*** strategy comprised of 4 key elements:

1. **Plan** – The measured risk strategy is always based on a plan, along with the Risk Manager's resolve to follow it.

2. **Data** – The plan design is based on data, evidence and research. Selection of product is a result, not the focus, of the plan.

3. **Time** – Asset allocation in the measured risk strategy is based on the length of time available for investments to grow before they are needed for consumption.

4. **Balance** – The measured risk strategy recognizes the best traits of the Systematic Withdrawal Technique and the Flooring Technique and combines them for balance and efficiency of income creation.

The Risk Manager's PRIM is constructed utilizing both drivers.

The Risk Manager's Basic Balanced PRIM

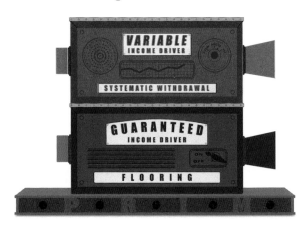

FUELING THE RISK MANAGER'S PRIM

The *Bucket System* is used to produce income for the Risk Manager.

RISK MANAGER

Buckets

The advantage of the Bucket System is that it allows you to integrate future income needs at specific future periods of time with how you allocate your assets. We call this strategy Consumption Allocated Investment Buckets. This means you will pick the appropriate investment tool (fixed annuity, bond, mutual fund, etc.) for the time horizon when you plan to consume the money. The technical term for planning income this way is called **Consumption-Based Asset Allocation.** This is a foundation of the Bucket System and will become clearer as we lay it out for you.

Research from one of the world's largest independent actuarial and consulting firms, Milliman, Inc., concludes that "indeed, at least two product categories, mutual funds and fixed indexed annuities ... will be required to maximize the sustainability of one's retirement income." This combination of mutual funds and fixed index annuities is the foundation of the Bucket System.

There are two steps to creating the Risk Manager's PRIM. First, determine your Income Floor and, second, fuel the Consumption Allocated Investment Buckets.

> "Consumption-based Asset Allocation introduces a new generation of asset management methodologies that utilize fundamental attributes of the investor, not the investment, as the primary determinant for all asset allocation decisions."
>
> THE FUTURE OF ASSET MANAGEMENT The Willis Group 2009

STEP #1 - DETERMINE YOUR INCOME FLOOR

First, you need to solve for your *Income Floor*, your *baseline income need*, and determine how much of your Fuel (Assets) you need to allocate to the Guaranteed Income Driver.

We will now assume that Maggie and Stan have mutated into Risk Managers, and they have set out to determine their *Income Floor* need by developing a spending budget.

There are many ways to calculate *Income Floor*, as it is a very personal thing. Some people may only cover fixed living expenses, such as the following:

- **Mortgage**
- **Taxes**
- **Food**
- **Gas/Electric/Water**
- **Insurances**
- **Credit Card Payments**
- **Auto/Gas**
- **Any other expenses that are a necessity**

Others may determine it is essential that they maintain a golf membership or pay dues for a club, and therefore those extra expenses will be part of their *Income Floor*.

Whatever the case may be for you, it is important to come up with a base number that needs to be guaranteed for you to have peace of mind about the future. This is the amount that will be generated by your Guaranteed Income Driver as your Income Floor.

Chart A below, shows that Social Security and pensions give Maggie and Stan $45,000 of fixed income. However, we know that their total required need is $85,000, leaving them $40,000 short.

After reviewing their baseline needs, they determine that they want an Income Floor of $75,000 and that they will get the balance of their income need, $10,000, from their Consumption Allocated Buckets. Since they already have $45,000 from their Social Security and Pension, they calculate that they are short $30,000. See **Chart B**.

Chart A

Current Fixed Income	Amount	
Social Security*	$	35,000
Pensions	$	10,000
Other	$	—
Total Current Fixed Income	$	**45,000**

Chart B

Income	Amount	
Required Total Income	$	85,000
Minimum Desired Income Floor	$	75,000
Current Fixed Income	$	**45,000**
Floor Income Gap to be Guaranteed	$	30,000
Measured Risk Income	$	10,000

CALCULATE ANNUITY PREMIUM NEEDED

Maggie and Stan now need to determine how much fuel they will need to fund their annuity. To do that they will need to divide the baseline need by the *INCOME FACTOR* based on their age(s):

TYPICAL INCOME FLOOR FACTORS

Age	Approximate Income Factor
60 – 65	0.50
66 – 70	.055
71 – 75	.060
76 – 80	.065

Note: Income Factors vary by product and may be higher or lower than the illustrated Factors above.

Maggie and Stan are 66-years-old, so they would make the following calculation to determine the amount of fuel (assets) needed for the fixed annuity to be included in their Income Floor:

$$\$30{,}000 / .055 = \$545{,}454$$

Maggie and Stan now know that they need to use $545,454 of their assets as fuel for their Guaranteed Income Driver. These funds serve to purchase a Fixed Annuity with an Income Rider that will pay $30,000 guaranteed for their lifetime. The combination of Social Security ($35,000), their pension ($10,000), and the annuity ($30,000) gives them an *Income Floor* of $75,000. Social Security grows over time with a cost-of-living adjustment (we have assumed 2%), therefore, the Income Floor grows over time as well.

> **NOTE:** To keep things simple, we're illustrating the fixed annuity floor income without increases over time. There are products that offer increasing income. We encourage you to compare those options with fixed payment income riders.

Risk Manager's Income Floor

INCOME FLOOR:
FA – Fixed Annuity   SS – Social Security   P – Pension

Fixed Annuity **$545,454**	FA **$30,000**	FA **$30,000**	FA **$30,000**	FA **$30,000**
PRE-FUELED INCOME	SS **$35,000** P **$10,000**	SS **$38,642** P **$10,000**	SS **$42,663** P **$10,000**	SS **$47,103** P **$10,000**
YEARLY INCOME FLOOR	**$75,000**/Year	**$78,642**/Year	**$82,663**/Year	**$87,103**/Year
TOTAL INCOME GOAL	**$85,000**/Year YEARS 1 – 5	**$98,538**/Year YEARS 6 – 10	**$114,233**/Year YEARS 11 – 15	**$132,427**/Year YEARS 16+

STEP #2 - FUND THE REMAINING CONSUMPTION ALLOCATED INVESTMENT BUCKETS

Use the remaining funds to fuel Buckets 1 – 4 using the *Consumption Allocated Investment Bucket Strategy* (investing assets to support income during specific future time periods). Note that while these buckets are fueled at the same time, they are accessed for income at different times in the future.

To simplify this example, we are going to assume 3% annual inflation but only give Maggie and Stan their Cost-of-Living adjustment every 5 years. By addressing inflation in this manner, it provides a clearer picture and understanding of inflation-adjusted income, allowing us to add the *Inflation Income Booster* to their PRIM.

Risk Manager's PRIM with Inflation Booster

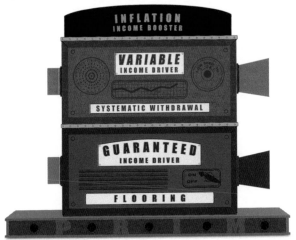

How do we determine how much fuel to put in buckets 1 – 4 and where to invest it? Take a look at the Total Income Growth in the next chart. That, plus some simple math, will make this much clearer.

Maggie and Stan plan to take $10,000 a year out of Bucket #1 for the next 5 years, which means they will need a lot of liquidity and almost no risk. They will want to place $50,000 in one or more of the following options:

- Money Market Fund
- Treasury Inflation Protected Securities (TIPS)
- Short term Investment-grade bonds

These choices offer a low yield, but they offer the most important features needed for this bucket: **safety and liquidity.**

Risk Manager's PRIM with Bucket #1 Fueled

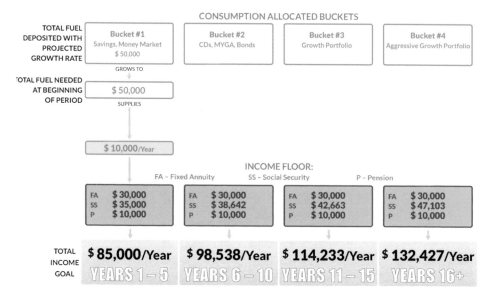

	Bucket #1	Bucket #2	Bucket #3	Bucket #4
CONSUMPTION ALLOCATED BUCKETS				
TOTAL FUEL DEPOSITED WITH PROJECTED GROWTH RATE	Savings, Money Market $50,000	CDs, MYGA, Bonds	Growth Portfolio	Aggressive Growth Portfolio

GROWS TO

TOTAL FUEL NEEDED AT BEGINNING OF PERIOD: $50,000

SUPPLIES

$10,000/Year

INCOME FLOOR:
FA – Fixed Annuity   SS – Social Security   P – Pension

FA	$30,000	FA	$30,000	FA	$30,000	FA	$30,000
SS	$35,000	SS	$38,642	SS	$42,663	SS	$47,103
P	$10,000	P	$10,000	P	$10,000	P	$10,000

TOTAL INCOME GOAL	$85,000/Year	$98,538/Year	$114,233/Year	$132,427/Year
	YEARS 1 – 5	YEARS 6 – 10	YEARS 11 – 15	YEARS 16+

Bucket #2 is funded with money that will not be needed for 5 years. This means they should lock in a guaranteed interest rate in a fixed product that will be fully liquid at the end of 5 years. Maggie & Stan will want to place $85,812 in the following:

- CDs
- Fixed Interest Annuity (Multi-Year Guaranteed Annuity or MYGA)
- Zero Coupon Bonds

We assume a 3% growth rate for the 5-year period during which

Maggie and Stan are growing the money. At the end of 5 years, they will have $99,480 liquid, which they can then spend down from years 6 to 10 at a rate of $19,896 per year.

Where did the $19,896 come from? Okay, some more math ...

To calculate a *cost-of-living adjustment* for years 6 – 10, we had to take $85,000 (the total income goal) and multiply that by 1.03 (3% inflation per year) 5 times to get their inflation-adjusted income goal of $98,538.

Now we must add an inflation-adjusted Social Security payment of $38,642 projected for year 6, $10,000 from the pension, and $30,000 from the annuity to get $78,642 for the year 6 income floor.

When you subtract the year 6 income floor ($78,642) from the year 6 inflation-adjusted income goal ($98,538), you arrive at the year 6 gap of $19,896. Which means we need a total of $99,480 ($19,896 x 5) at the beginning of year 6.

Using a fixed interest rate (3%) that is guaranteed, we can easily calculate that $85,812 is needed today to grow to the $99,480 needed in 5 years. This is what their program looks like now:

Risk Manager's PRIM with Bucket #2 Fueled

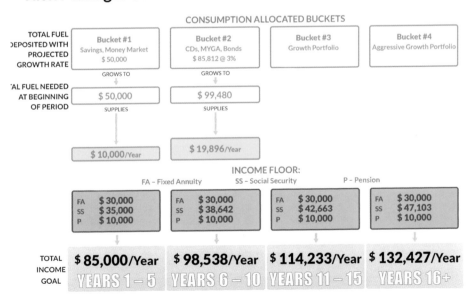

Utilizing a fixed interest rate product for this bucket, combined with money market funds in Bucket #2, minimizes Sequence of Return Risk for a full decade after Maggie and Stan's retirement.

Two more Buckets to go.

Bucket #3 is funded using the same math principles, but this time the money will not be needed for 10 years, which means we can take measured risk in the market.

To give Maggie and Stan a Cost-of-Living Adjustment for years 11 – 15, we had to take $85,000 and multiply it by 1.03 (3%) 10 times to get their inflation-adjusted income goal of $114,233.

Maggie and Stan add up their inflation-adjusted Social Security payment of $42,663 projected for year 11, $10,000 from the pension, and $30,000 from the annuity to get $82,663 for the year 11 income floor.

If you subtract the year 11 income floor ($82,663) from the year 11 inflation-adjusted income goal ($114,233) you arrive at the year 11 gap of $31,570. Which means we need a total of $157,850 ($31,570 x 5) at the beginning of year 11.

Maggie and Stan will want to place $90,906 in the following:

- 50/50 mix of stock and bond mutual funds.

The *Market Holding Period* is the length of time between an asset's purchase and sale. The longer the holding period,the higher the chance of achieving your investment goals.

This choice gives us the ability to take advantage of a long market holding period. Research shows that the longer you are invested in the stock market, the greater opportunity you have to reach your investment goals. Take a look at the chart on the next page showing positive and negative returns from 1926 through 2015. It shows that if you held your money in the S&P 500 for any 20 year period, you would have experienced a gain 100% of the time. However, if you invested for only a day, there was a 46% chance you would lose money. By committing to a ten year holding period in a 50/50 portfolio, you are playing the odds (94% historically) that you will have positive results. Therefore, we can use a *projected* average return of 5%, which would grow to $157,850 over the full 10-year period from the time they make the investment.

S&P 500: 1926 – 2015

Time Frame	Positive	Negative
Daily	54%	46%
Quarterly	68%	32%
One Year	74%	26%
5 Years	86%	14%
10 Years	94%	6%
20 years	100%	0%

Source: Returns 2.0

When they get to year 11, they can take the $157,850 and move it to a safe, liquid place like they had in Bucket #2. They will then draw down those funds to provide income for years 11 – 15.

Risk Manager's PRIM with Bucket #3 Fueled

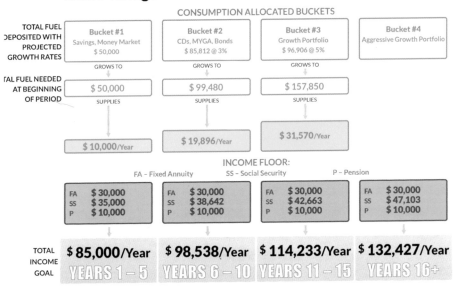

Bucket #4 is used for long-term growth and is able to take advantage of a much longer holding period in the market. It will help us keep up with inflation and build a buffer for emergencies or a change of plans. Therefore, Maggie and Stan can take measured risk by placing the rest of their money ($221,828) in the following:

CONSUMPTION ALLOCATED BUCKETS

	Bucket #1	Bucket #2	Bucket #3	Bucket #4
TOTAL FUEL DEPOSITED WITH PROJECTED GROWTH RATES	Savings, Money Market $50,000	CDs, MYGA, Bonds $85,812 @ 3%	Growth Portfolio $96,906 @ 5%	Aggressive Growth Portfolio $221,828 @ 8%
	GROWS TO	GROWS TO	GROWS TO	GROWS TO
TOTAL FUEL NEEDED AT BEGINNING OF PERIOD	$50,000	$99,480	$157,850	$703,675
	SUPPLIES	SUPPLIES	SUPPLIES	SUPPLIES
	$10,000/Year	$19,896/Year	$31,570/Year	$45,324/Year

INCOME FLOOR:
FA – Fixed Annuity   SS – Social Security   P – Pension

	Bucket #1	Bucket #2	Bucket #3	Bucket #4
FA	$30,000	$30,000	$30,000	$30,000
SS	$35,000	$38,642	$42,663	$47,103
P	$10,000	$10,000	$10,000	$10,000

TOTAL INCOME GOAL	$85,000/Year	$98,538/Year	$114,233/Year	$132,427/Year
	YEARS 1 – 5	YEARS 6 – 10	YEARS 11 – 15	YEARS 16+

Understand that the Risk Manager's PRIM can be built more conservatively with additional buckets, or more aggressively with fewer fixed products according to your personal taste. Additionally, to keep things simple, we did not credit any interest during the payout phase of each bucket. You could reasonably expect to earn 1% – 3% per year on funds waiting to be paid out during any 5-year period. This would mean less money would be required for the earlier buckets, and more funds could be deposited in Bucket #5.

> The Risk Manager's PRIM has the flexibility to be built more conservatively or more aggressively according to your Risk Style.

However, they are not done adding parts. The Sequence of Returns Booster can be added, because they have eliminated that risk by utilizing fixed instruments for income early in their retirement. Additionally, they can add the Longevity Warranty because they are generating income that will last as long as they do.

The Risk Manager's PRIM performs exceptionally well in both up and down markets. Their inflation-adjusted income goal is met for life, and they have growth opportunities in their long-term buckets. Additionally, all the retirement income risks are covered:

- Longevity Risk—income will last as long as they do.
- Excess Withdrawal Risk—they have set up *consumption-based* asset allocation buckets, providing a planned withdrawal strategy.
- Inflation Risk—income is adjusted every 5 years to keep up with cost of living.
- Sequence of Return Risk—is minimized and pushed out a full decade.

With all the Buckets filled with fuel, the Risk Manager's PRIM looks like a highly productive income machine:

THE RISK MANAGER'S PRIM AND THE UNCERTAINTY ZONE

As you would imagine, the uncertainty zone for the Risk Manager falls in between that of the Risk Taker and the Risk Avoider. Its balanced approach between guaranteed and measured risk fulfills the Risk Manager's middle of the road approach to risk.

RISK TAKER'S
UNCERTAINTY ZONE

RISK MANAGER'S
UNCERTAINTY
ZONE

RISK AVOIDER'S
UNCERTAINTY ZONE

RISK TAKER'S
UNCERTAINTY ZONE

READY FOR ACTION!

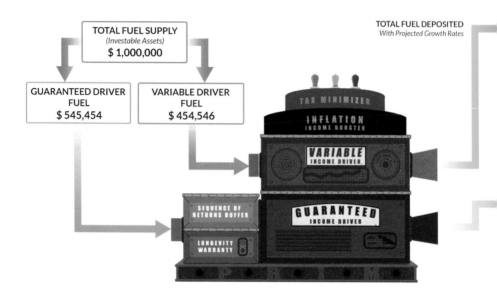

WHAT ABOUT TAXES?

Income Sequencing is the strategy for selecting the sequence of withdrawing funds from savings vehicles during retirement.

Your Income Drivers will be fueled with a combination of qualified funds (pre-tax money held in retirement related accounts) and non-qualified funds (any after-tax money held outside of retirement accounts). You will need to choose which funds to use early and which funds to draw down later in life. This is called **Income Sequencing:** the strategy for selecting the sequence of withdrawing funds from savings vehicles during retirement.

For example, should you program your drivers to withdraw funds from the taxable account first, then the traditional IRA, and lastly your ROTH? Or would another sequence be preferable?

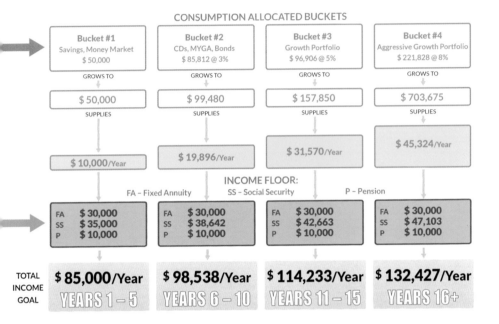

CONSUMPTION ALLOCATED BUCKETS

Bucket #1	Bucket #2	Bucket #3	Bucket #4
Savings, Money Market	CDs, MYGA, Bonds	Growth Portfolio	Aggressive Growth Portfolio
$ 50,000	$ 85,812 @ 3%	$ 96,906 @ 5%	$ 221,828 @ 8%
GROWS TO	GROWS TO	GROWS TO	GROWS TO
$ 50,000	$ 99,480	$ 157,850	$ 703,675
SUPPLIES	SUPPLIES	SUPPLIES	SUPPLIES
$ 10,000/Year	$ 19,896/Year	$ 31,570/Year	$ 45,324/Year

INCOME FLOOR:

FA – Fixed Annuity   SS – Social Security   P – Pension

FA $ 30,000	FA $ 30,000	FA $ 30,000	FA $ 30,000
SS $ 35,000	SS $ 38,642	SS $ 42,663	SS $ 47,103
P $ 10,000	P $ 10,000	P $ 10,000	P $ 10,000

TOTAL INCOME GOAL

$ 85,000/Year	$ 98,538/Year	$ 114,233/Year	$ 132,427/Year
YEARS 1 – 5	YEARS 6 – 10	YEARS 11 – 15	YEARS 16+

The conventional rule of thumb is that you should withdraw funds from taxable accounts before you take funds from tax-deferred qualified retirement accounts. The thinking is that by delaying use of 401ks or IRAs, for example, the compounding effect of tax-deferral will produce higher values in the future.

While this may sound logical, there are many exceptions. Here are some things to keep in mind:

- Time the withdrawal of funds from qualified accounts for those years when you are in a lower tax bracket.

- Be careful of the years when there are Required Minimum Distributions (RMDs) at age 70 ½ and beyond. If you have a substantial amount of assets in these accounts, your RMDs could drive you into a much higher tax bracket. In that case, it would be better to reduce the amount in these accounts by taking withdrawals from them earlier in retirement.

- Keep an eye on taxes. Every dollar withdrawn from a tax-deferred account is a taxable event. If taxes are cycling higher, it would benefit you to take these funds now, when taxes are lower.

- Finally, if you have tax-free money available through a ROTH or through a LIRP (Life Insurance Retirement Plan), use these funds judiciously to keep your income in the lowest tax brackets or below a needed threshold.

THE PROS AND CONS OF THE RISK MANAGER'S APPROACH

The Pros are:

- Efficiently integrates timing of consumption-need with appropriate asset allocation.

- Combines a guaranteed floor of income along with inflation-adjusted income to help maintain purchasing power.

- Minimizes the impact of emotions by creating a systematic process for income and asset maximization that is not based on fear of arbitrary or poor decision making.

- Since some assets are dedicated towards guaranteed income, it allows other assets to be earmarked for more aggressive growth.

- Eliminates the Retirement Income Risks—Longevity Risk, Inflation Risk, Excess Withdrawal Risk, and Sequence of Return Risk.

- Increases holding periods on equities to realize the best possible chance of achieving projected market returns.

- Assures asset liquidity to produce income in tax-efficient sequences when needed at specific periods of time.

The Cons are:

- Transitioning from one bucket to another could require attention or assistance from a financial professional.

- Does not take advantage of the full upside potential of the markets as compared to the systematic withdrawal approach.

- Less money is fully liquid.

- This is a more complex system, and declining cognitive abilities could hamper the ability to manage the plan and investments over time.

Chapter 8 Wrap-Up

☐ The Bucket system is used to produce different types of income at different periods of time.

☐ You must determine your *baseline income need.*

☐ Fund the Income Floor with a fixed annuity. Calculate premium needed by dividing the *baseline need* by an *income factor.*

☐ Fund buckets 1 – 4 using consumption-based asset allocation.

☐ Simplify adjusting for inflation (Cost of Living) by adjusting income for every five year period instead of for every year.

☐ Bucket #1 is invested in very safe products and is consumed years 1 – 5.

☐ Bucket #2 is invested in a 5 year CDs, MYGA, or Zero Coupon Bonds for guaranteed growth which is completely liquid after 5 years and consumed years 6 – 10.

☐ Bucket #3 is invested in a 50/50 stock and bond mutual fund for 10 years and consumed years 11 – 15 after it has been moved to a fixed account.

☐ Bucket #4 is invested in an 80/20 to 100/0 stock & bond mutual fund for 15+ years and the process continues.

☐ The Bucket strategy can be built more conservatively or more aggressively according to personal taste.

☐ Taxes require special consideration to minimize their effect and maximize income.

☐ **All Retirement Income Risks are solved.**

UNDER THE HOOD OF YOUR PRIM

9

Maggie and Stan have designed their PRIM, made sure all the parts work well with other parts, planned their outcomes, and calculated the appropriate amount of fuel required for each income outcome. When they turn their PRIM on, two things happen immediately:

1. Their Guaranteed Income Driver is programmed to create the *Income Floor*—a combination of Social Security, Pensions and selected annuities. An annuity is required to fill the gap when Social Security and Pensions do not provide sufficient income to meet the income floor goal.

2. The Variable Income Driver is programmed with an investment methodology which determine how these funds will be managed.

Under the hood of their PRIM, there is a lot going on in terms of selection processes and market investment strategies. If either are poorly executed, Maggie and Stan won't get the results they are looking for.

Once again, it is not the scope of this book to teach you the specifics of fixed annuities or about the many different investment options and strategies available. We feel, however, that it is worth noting how important it will be that you approach the selection process wisely, and that we give you some ideas of our approach and what the evidence indicates.

CHOOSING YOUR ANNUITY

Like ice cream, fixed annuities come in all shapes and sizes with a variety of toppings for you to consider. Here's our basic annuity checklist:

ANNUITY CONSIDERATION	COMMENT
Length or Term of the Contract	We like to stay in the 7 – 10 year range for Fixed Index Annuities (FIA). This is where you can generally get your best deal—a balance of growth potential and flexibility.
Fees	Many Fixed Annuities do not have any annual fees at all (other than surrender charges if you cash in your annuity prematurely). And, they are often confused with Variable Annuities, where fees can run as high as 3.5% – 4.0%. We do, however, consider using annuities with a fee if it offers a special kind of income rider that is the best fit for our client's circumstances.
Indexing Options	Indexing options are the mathematical formulas that determine how much interest is credited to your annuity when the market rises (there are never any losses when the market falls). We prefer annuities with multiple options from which we can choose each year as the markets shift and change. We also prefer annuities that offer an uncapped strategy (formula) i.e. if the S&P went up 15%, your annuity would be credited with 15% minus what is called a "spread." Let's say the spread is 2.0%, then you would earn 15% – 2% or 13% for that year.
Income Riders	Some annuities have a fee associated with their Income Riders; and some don't. And, some annuities have options for increasing income; and some don't. We prefer annuities with low or no charges for their income rider; and we prefer annuities that have a rising income option. While these are our immediate preferences, in many circumstances, and with certain Risk Styles, other types of income riders may work better.
Death Benefit	The question always arises about what happens if you pass away prematurely. All Fixed Index Annuities provide, at minimum, that the assets remaining at death (after income is withdrawn) will pass to your heirs without any surrender charges or any other penalties and fees that may otherwise be associated with the distribution. We prefer FIAs that have an enhanced death benefit, especially when it is offered at no cost.
Insurance Carrier Rating	We prefer carriers that have an A- rating or better.

CHOOSING HOW YOUR MONEY IS MANAGED

The challenge for most investors is how to decipher through the bevvy of theories, opinions and beliefs on the best way to invest in the stock market.

The Variable Income Driver can be a challenge to program. The challenge for most investors, is how to decipher the bevvy of theories, opinions, and beliefs on the best way to invest in the stock market. All one needs to do is turn on the TV or radio, thumb through a magazine or newspaper, buy the latest "how to invest" newsletter, or just Google "how to invest," and you will receive an overwhelming amount of information. Almost everyone, it seems, has a different approach to making money in the market.

We use research and evidence to cut through all the hyperbole about how best to make money in the market. The evidence is clear about three important points, points that you should keep in mind when you are interviewing advisors or money managers to watch over your money.

The Evidence Says:

1. It is impossible to try and time the market and do so consistently over a long period of time.

> "Oh, sure, you could try to time the market by selling now, waiting for it to bottom, and buying back. A lot of people get rich doing this in novels … You know why they're able to do this? Because the authors get to cheat."
>
> You Can't Time the Market Bloomberg View Megan McArdle 8.24.15

2. All too often the market moves with no rhyme or reason. It is, above all, unpredictable. Those who claim success in market

timing, trying to figure out when to buy and when to sell, generally underperform other modes of managing money.

Based on the evidence, we suggest you steer away from money management that is "active" in nature (or place a much smaller percentage of your assets with these managers). As well, those funds that try and time the market are typically far more expensive than other modes of investing.

In the chart below you can see that in the short-run, active funds do better than their benchmarks. However, in the longer run, just five years in this example, almost 90% no longer beat the same benchmarks.

Percentage of Funds that Fail to Match/Beat Benchmarks
As of June 30, 2014

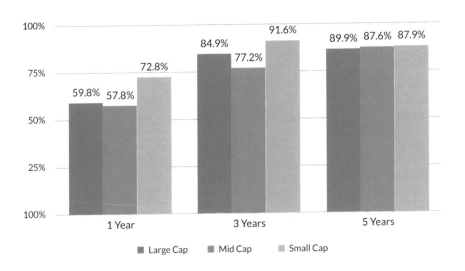

2. Fees and Costs matter.

Keep in mind that there are fees which are easily recognizable, and there are fees buried below the surface that you may not be aware of. Funds that use timing strategies tend to be far higher in both their observable and hidden fees than, for example, index funds.

When choosing your advisor, make sure that he or she reviews *all* the fees and costs, because they matter greatly. This chart will give you an idea of just how critically important they are in determining your outcome. In this example, the difference between a 1% expense ratio and a 2.5% expense ratio over 30 years is $2,561,174. Since active management is usually more expensive (due to the level of trading within the portfolio), it must perform at much higher levels to justify the cost. Unfortunately, the data proves it does not.

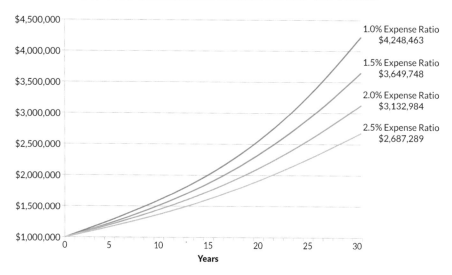

Impact of Expense Ratio
On 6% Annualized Return Over 30 Years

PASSIVE MONEY MANAGEMENT— MODERN PORTFOLIO THEORY

Passive investors today formulate their investing style based on Modern Portfolio Theory (MPT) and, typically, use low cost index funds or exchange traded funds (ETFs).

MPT is a theory pioneered in 1952 by Nobel Prize winning economist Harry Markowitz. Markowitz proposed that you could construct a portfolio made up of multiple asset classes that will maximize returns and minimize risk for any given growth goal.

Every portfolio is highly diversified and engineered in such a way (based on how each asset class works or correlates with the other assets classes) to be "efficient". By connecting a line through each efficient portfolio, an "efficient frontier" of optimal portfolios offering the maximum possible expected return for any given level of risk is created.

The Efficient Frontier

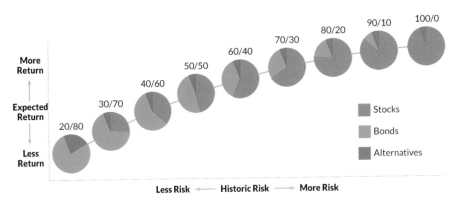

Referencing the Efficient Frontier, you can see the only way to increase return is to also increase risk. As Risk Managers, Maggie and Stan will choose a portfolio of mid-range risk. Their choice will then determine the projected growth of their portfolio based on its position on the Efficient Frontier.

Passive investors count on the market rising over time, and historically that is exactly what has happened. It is for this reason that they ignore market cycles and never try to time the market as an active investor would.

The Market Rises Over Time

A *passive strategy* takes the emotion out of the equation.

MODERN PORTFOLIO THEORY AND FORWARD LOOKING RETURNS

MPT has evolved since its creation in 1952. Originally developed primarily looking at historical returns. MPT managers today realize that while looking back in history is a good indicator, there is also a need to look forward and tactically adjust asset class percentages to reflect the current state of the markets. These managers are sometimes called strategic money managers.

An industry research group, The Tactical Think Tank, determined that by adding a *forward looking* element to the development of portfolio construction, more precise asset class percentages can be determined.

> "The use of forward-looking returns has a meaningful impact on how we build portfolios. The inputs used for each class (expected returns, volatility, and correlations) impact how much we allocate to each asset class."
>
> Savant Capital Management — Savant Backstage — Forward-Looking Returns "A Smart, But Humble Approach" 2010

Perhaps the most important point in considering portfolio management is to be realistic about what you know and what you don't know. The Variable Income Driver, with assets invested in the market, delivers uncertain results. Moreover, we have also seen that the uncertain results of the Variable Income Driver are more disparate than that of the Guaranteed Income Driver.

Modern Portfolio Theory, with a Forward-Looking Overlay, is a research based approach that provides a modern, engineered portfolio designed to yield the highest return at the lowest risk, lowering the uncertainty associated with this driver. For Maggie and Stan, they now know the best program for their Variable Income Driver.

Chapter 9 Wrap-Up

- ☐ There are many theories, opinions, and beliefs about the best way to manage money invested in the market.

- ☐ The idea of making money in the market by buying low and selling high is impossible to execute because it is impossible to time the market consistently over a period of time.

- ☐ Fear and greed affect individual investors which trigger emotional reactions which often lead to do the poor decision making i.e. buying high and selling low instead of buying low and selling high.

- ☐ Evidence shows that an active investing strategy does not work well in the long term.

- ☐ Passive investing, using low-cost index funds or ETFs, relies on the fact that markets will rise over time.

- ☐ Modern Portfolio Theory engineers portfolios using a wide diversification of index funds covering all asset classes. These are blended together in a way to maximize gain and minimize risk for each type of portfolio.

- ☐ The Efficient Frontier is a set of efficient portfolios for different growth and risk levels connected by a line.

- ☐ Modern Portfolio Theory today employs a tactical element called Forward Looking Returns, which adjust asset percentages based on current market and economic conditions.

- ☐ Evidence clearly shows that MTP combined with Forward Looking Returns offers the highest and most consistent returns, at the lowest risk, over the longest periods of time.

- ☐ MPT with Forward Looking Returns carry the lowest costs and fees of virtually all investing methods.

CHAPTER 10

A FEW FINAL WORDS

10

When you consider the future, do you see the proverbial glass half-full or half-empty?

Our hope is that PRIM methodology will make you more confident about your future, and in that way, when you look at the glass you will see it as half-full, or better yet, flowing over the top. But nothing happens unless you do something about it. We are reminded of a quote from a 19th century philosopher, Herbert Spencer:

The great aim of education is not knowledge but action.

It tells us that reading about PRIM is quite different than building one and experiencing the magic of knowing that your retirement income and your quality of life is safe and secure.

Another quote we'd like to share with you is from Hugh Mackay, an Australian psychologist and researcher. He was a realist and saw life and human beings this way:

Nothing is perfect. Life is messy. Relationships are complex. Outcomes are uncertain. People are irrational.

Here's the point.

Assuming you take action and build your PRIM, what happens then? After all, few things work out exactly as we plan them. We set things in motion, aiming at a specific goal, but along the way we are buffered by events and thrown off course. Even the technologically sophisticated Apollo moon rockets were off course 97% of the time (yes, they were). With wise adjustments along the way, however, they reached their goal with pin-point accuracy.

In the world of PRIM, the same is true.

Once you flip the start switch on your PRIM, it will hum along creating a flow of cash for you to spend for the rest of your life. However, along your retirement journey you may get buffered or downright shoved off course. The storms could come in the form of a market collapse bigger than you thought possible; a family member in need of being bailed out of a tough jam; inflation could take off like it did in the 1980's when it was 14% – 16% per year; the grandkids might need money for college; or that second home you enjoy so much gets wiped out by a hurricane.

Whatever it is, your PRIM will help you stay on course, and with some minor adjustments, like the Apollo rocket, you too will reach your goals, sometimes with pin-point accuracy.

At the beginning of this book we talked about **Sleeping Well on Windy Nights**. We expressed that life is not about a lump sum of money, which is simply fuel for your journey. We believe that your end-goal is a good quality of life with peace of mind. PRIM was de-signed to fulfill those goals. Put your PRIM together carefully, and it will deliver what you seek—today, tomorrow, and thereafter.

Build your PRIM—enjoy your journey!

FURTHER READING EVIDENCE

- Evaluating Investments versus Insurance in Retirement, Wade Pfau, Advisor Perspectives
- Market Risk, Mortality Risk, and Sustainable Retirement Asset Allocation: A Downside Risk Perspective, W.V. Harlow & Keith C. Brown
- NRRI Update Shows Half Still Falling Short, Alicia H. Munnell, Wenliang Hou, and Anthony Webb, Center for Retirement Research at Boston College
- Optimal Retirement Income Solutions in DC Retirement Plans, Steve Vernon, Wade Pfau, Joe Tomlinson, Society of Actuaries
- Planning With Certainty: A New Strategy for Retirement Income, Milliman Inc.
- Changing Face of Private Retirement Plans, Jack VanDerhei, Employee Benefit Research Institute
- Diminishing Returns: Why Investors May Need to Lower Their Expectations, McKinsey Global Institute
- Investing Your Lump Sum at Retirement, David Babbel, Craig B. Merrill, Wharton Financial Institutions Center

Made in the USA
Lexington, KY
29 July 2017